SUPREME COURT NOMINATIONS 1789 - 2005: ACTIONS (INCLUDING SPEED) BY THE SENATE, THE JUDICIARY COMMITTEE, AND THE PRESIDENT

Supreme Court Nominations 1789 - 2005: Actions (Including Speed) by the Senate, the Judiciary Committee, and the President

Denis Steven Rutkus
Maureen Bearden
and
R. Sam Garrett

Nova Science Publishers, Inc.
New York

For permission to use material from this book please contact us:
Telephone 631-231-7269; Fax 631-231-8175
Web Site: http://www.novapublishers.com

NOTICE TO THE READER

Library of Congress Cataloging-in-Publication Data

Supreme Court nominations 1789-2005 : actions (including speed) by the Senate, the Judiciary Committee, and the President / Denis Steven Rutkus, Maureen Bearden and Sam Garrett (editor[s]).
p. cm.
Includes index.
ISBN 1-60021-354-5
1. United States. Supreme Court--Officials and employees--Selection and appointment--History. 2. Judges--Selection and appointment--United States--History. I. Rutkus, Denis Steven. II. Bearden, Maureen. III. Garrett, Sam.
KF8742.S87 2006
347.73'2634--dc22 2006022226

Published by Nova Science Publishers, Inc. ✢New York

CONTENTS

PREFACE

The process of appointing Supreme Court Justices has undergone changes over two centuries, but its most basic feature - the sharing of power between the President and Senate - has remained unchanged. To receive a lifetime appointment to the Court, a candidate must first be nominated by the President and then confirmed by the Senate. An important role also has come to be played midway in the process (after the President selects, but before the Senate considers) by the Senate Judiciary Committee. This book provides information on the amount of time taken to act on all Supreme Court nominations occurring between 1900 and the present. It focuses on the actual amounts of time that Presidents and the Senate have taken to act (as opposed to the elapsed time between official points in the process). This book focuses on when the Senate became aware of the President's selection (e.g., via a public announcement by the President).

The process of appointing Supreme Court Justices has undergone changes over two centuries, but its most basic feature — the sharing of power between the President and Senate — has remained unchanged. To receive a lifetime appointment to the Court, a candidate must first be nominated by the President and then confirmed by the Senate. An important role also has come to be played midway in the process (after the President selects, but before the Senate considers) by the Senate Judiciary Committee. Table 1 of chapter 1 lists and describes actions taken by the Senate, the Senate Judiciary Committee, and the President on all Supreme Court nominations, from 1789 to the present. The table provides the name of each person nominated to the Court and the name of the President making the nomination. It also tracks the dates of formal actions taken, and time elapsing between these actions, by the Senate or Senate Judiciary Committee on each nomination, starting with the date that the Senate received the nomination from the President. For another perspective on Supreme Court nominations, focusing, among other things, on when the Senate first *became aware* of each President's nominee selections (e.g.,via public announcements of the President). Thirty-nine of the 42 Presidents in the history of the United States have made a total of 158 nominations to the Supreme Court, and the Senate has confirmed 121 of them (with one now pending before the Senate). Of the 36 unsuccessful nominations, 11 were rejected in Senate roll-call votes, while nearly all of the rest, in the face of committee or Senate opposition to the nominee or the President, were withdrawn by the President, or were postponed, tabled, or never voted on by the Senate. A total of 114 of the 158 nominations were referred to a Senate committee, with 113 of them to the Judiciary Committee (including almost all nominations since 1868). Prior to 1916, the Judiciary Committee considered Supreme Court nominations behind closed doors. Since 1946, however, almost all nominees have received public confirmation hearings. Most recent hearings have lasted four or more days. Since 1967, a median of 37 days elapsed between the Senate's receipt of a Supreme Court nomination and a final committee vote. The Senate has confirmed about three-quarters of the 157 nominations it has received since 1789 (not including the pending 158th nomination), with 11 rejected in roll-call votes, 11 withdrawn by the President, and 14 lapsed at the end of a session of Congress.

The speed with which appointments to the Supreme Court move through various stages in the nomination-and-confirmation process is often of great interest to all parties directly involved and the nation as a whole. Shortly after President George W. Bush's October 3, 2005, announcement of White House Counsel Harriet E. Miers as his nominee to replace Associate Justice Sandra Day O'Connor on the Court, both the President and the majority leader of the Senate advocated that the Senate should vote on her nomination "by Thanksgiving" (i.e., within 52 days of the announcement). Senate Judiciary Committee Chairman Arlen Specter stated that he would like to see confirmation hearings on the nomination concluded by Thanksgiving. Chapter 2 provides information on the amount of time taken to act on all Supreme Court nominations occurring between 1900 and the present. It focuses on the *actual* amounts of time that Presidents and the Senate have taken to act (as opposed to the elapsed time between *official* points in the process). For example, rather than starting the nomination clock with the official notification of the President of a forthcoming vacancy (e.g., via receipt of a formal retirement letter), this report focuses on when the President first *learned* of a Justice's intention to leave the Court (e.g., via a private conversation with the outgoing Justice), or received word that a sitting Justice had died. Likewise, rather than starting the confirmation clock with the transmission of the official nomination to the Senate, this report focuses on when the Senate *became aware* of the President's selection (e.g., via a public announcement by the President). The data indicate that the entire nomination-and-confirmation process (from when the President first learned of a vacancy to final Senate action) has generally taken almost twice as long for nominees after 1980 than for nominees in the previous 80 years. From 1900 to 1980, the entire process took a median of 59 days; from 1981 through 2005, the process took a median of 113 days. Although Presidents after 1980 have moved more quickly than their predecessors in announcing nominees after learning of vacancies (a median of 18 days compared with 34 days before 1980), the Senate portion of the process (i.e., from the nomination announcement to final Senate action) now appears to take much longer than before (a median of 84 days from 1981 through 2005, compared with 28 days from 1900 through 1980). Most notably, the amount of time between the nomination announcement and first Judiciary Committee hearing has more than tripled — from a median of 13 days (1900-1980) to 51 days (1981-2005). These data suggest that, if recent past experience is a guide, it may be difficult for the Senate to complete action on the Miers nomination by Thanksgiving. However, there is substantial variation within these summary statistics; every nomination has its own pace. For example, Senate consideration of the nomination of Ruth Bader Ginsberg in 1993 took 50 days after the presidential announcement. If the Miers nomination followed that pace, Senate action could be completed by Thanksgiving.

Chapter 1

SUPREME COURT NOMINATIONS, 1789 - 2005: ACTIONS BY THE SENATE, THE JUDICIARY COMMITTEE, AND THE PRESIDENT*

Denis Steven Rutkus and Maureen Bearden

ABSTRACT

The process of appointing Supreme Court Justices has undergone changes over two centuries, but its most basic feature — the sharing of power between the President and Senate — has remained unchanged. To receive a lifetime appointment to the Court, a candidate must first be nominated by the President and then confirmed by the Senate. An important role also has come to be played midway in the process (after the President selects, but before the Senate considers) by the Senate Judiciary Committee.

Table 1 of this report lists and describes actions taken by the Senate, the Senate Judiciary Committee, and the President on all Supreme Court nominations, from 1789 to the present. The table provides the name of each person nominated to the Court and the name of the President making the nomination. It also tracks the dates of formal actions taken, and time elapsing between these actions, by the Senate or Senate Judiciary Committee on each nomination, starting with the date that the Senate received the nomination from the President. For another perspective on Supreme Court nominations, focusing, among other things, on when the Senate first *became aware* of each President's nominee selections (e.g.,via public announcements of the

---

* Excerpted from CRS Report Order Code RL33225, dated January 5, 2006.

President), see CRS Report RL33118, *Speed of Presidential and Senate Actions on Supreme Court Nominations, 1900-2005*, by R. Sam Garrett, Denis Steven Rutkus, and Curtis W. Copeland.

Thirty-nine of the 42 Presidents in the history of the United States have made a total of 158 nominations to the Supreme Court, and the Senate has confirmed 121 of them (with one now pending before the Senate). Of the 36 unsuccessful nominations, 11 were rejected in Senate roll-call votes, while nearly all of the rest, in the face of committee or Senate opposition to the nominee or the President, were withdrawn by the President, or were postponed, tabled, or never voted on by the Senate. A total of 114 of the 158 nominations were referred to a Senate committee, with 113 of them to the Judiciary Committee (including almost all nominations since 1868). Prior to 1916, the Judiciary Committee considered Supreme Court nominations behind closed doors. Since 1946, however, almost all nominees have received public confirmation hearings. Most recent hearings have lasted four or more days. Since 1967, a median of 37 days elapsed between the Senate's receipt of a Supreme Court nomination and a final committee vote. The Senate has confirmed about three-quarters of the 157 nominations it has received since 1789 (not including the pending 158th nomination), with 11 rejected in roll-call votes, 11 withdrawn by the President, and 14 lapsed at the end of a session of Congress.

INTRODUCTION

The procedure for appointing a Justice to the Supreme Court of the United States is provided for by the Constitution in only a few words. The "Appointments Clause" (Article II, Section 2, clause 2) states that the President "shall nominate, and by and with the Advice and Consent of the Senate, shall appoint ... Judges of the supreme Court." The process of appointing Justices has undergone changes over two centuries, but its most basic feature — the sharing of power between the President and Senate — has remained unchanged. To receive a lifetime appointment to the Court, a candidate must first be nominated by the President and then confirmed by the Senate. An important role also has come to be played midway in the process (after the President selects, but before the Senate considers) by the Senate Judiciary Committee.

On rare occasions, Presidents also have made Supreme Court appointments without the Senate's consent, when the Senate was in recess. Such "recess appointments," however, were temporary, with their terms expiring at the end of the Senate's next session. The last recess appointments to the Court were made in the 1950s.

The appointment of a Supreme Court Justice might or might not proceed smoothly. From the first appointments in 1789, the Senate has confirmed 121 out of 157 Court nominations, with a 158th now pending before the Senate.[1] Of the 36 unsuccessful nominations, 11 were rejected in Senate roll-call votes, while nearly all of the rest, in the face of committee or Senate opposition to the nominee or the President, were withdrawn by the President, or were postponed, tabled, or never voted on by the Senate.

DESCRIPTION OF REPORT'S CONTENTS

This report lists and describes actions taken by the Senate, the Senate Judiciary Committee, and the President on all Supreme Court nominations, from 1789 to the present. The listing appears in a Supreme Court nominations table, Table 1, later in this report. Preceding the table is summary text, which highlights certain nominations statistics derived from the table. The text also provides historical background information on the Supreme Court appointment process and uses nominations statistics from the table to shed light on ways in which the appointment process has evolved over time. Many of the statistical findings discussed, for example, provide historical perspective on the emergence, and then increased involvement, of the Senate Judiciary Committee in the appointment process.

Specifically, the table lists, for each Supreme Court nomination, the following:

- name of the person nominated (the nominee);
- name of the President who made the nomination;
- date the nomination was received in the Senate;
- date(s) of any committee hearings held on the nomination that were open to the public;
- type and date of final committee action; and
- type and date of final action by the Senate or, in rarer instances, by the President (when the final action taken on a nomination was its withdrawal by the President).

Table 1 also shows the speed with which action was taken on each nomination, specifically presenting the number of days that elapsed from the date the nomination was formally received in the Senate until the following:

- the first day of public confirmation hearings (if any);
- the date of final committee action (if any); and
- the date of final Senate action or presidential withdrawal of the nomination.

The table also lists all recess appointments to the Supreme Court, as well as the later nomination of each recess appointee.

Table 1, in sum, tracks the dates of formal actions taken by the Senate or Senate Judiciary Committee on each Supreme Court nomination, starting with the date that the Senate received the nomination from the President. For another perspective on Supreme Court nominations, focusing, among other things, on when the Senate informally first *became aware* of each President's nominee selections (e.g., via public announcements of the President), see CRS Report RL33118, *Speed of Presidential and Senate Actions on Supreme Court Nominations, 1900-2005*, by R. Sam Garrett, Denis Steven Rutkus, and Curtis W. Copeland.

Actions by the full Senate tracked in Table 1 are those on which the Senate took *final* action (ordinarily in the form of confirmation, and less often in the form of rejecting, tabling, or postponing action on a nomination). For certain Supreme Court nominations, Table 1 also provides dates of procedural actions taken on the Senate floor, prior to or after final Senate action, in order to put the final action in fuller context. The table, however, does not account for all Senate procedural actions on, or for all dates of Senate floor consideration of, Supreme Court nominations.

Findings from the Nominations Table

Number of Nominations and Nominees

Table 1 lists all 158 Supreme Court nominations since 1789, including the pending nomination of Samuel A. Alito Jr. Each of the 158 nominations entailed a President signing a nomination message, which was then transmitted to, and received by, the Senate. A lesser number of separate individuals, 139, were actually nominated to the Court, with some of them nominated more than once.[2]

Of the 158 total nominations to the Court, 22 were to the position of Chief Justice and the other 136 to a position as Associate Justice. The 22 Chief Justice nominations involved 20 persons nominated once, and one person nominated twice.[3] The 136 Associate Justice nominations involved 119 persons nominated once, seven persons nominated twice, and one person nominated three times.

Presidents Who Made the Nominations

Thirty-nine of the 42 Presidents in the history of the United States have made nominations to the Supreme Court.[4] These 39 are listed in the second column of Table 1. All but one of the 39 Presidents succeeded in having at least one Supreme Court nomination receive Senate confirmation. The one exception was President Andrew Johnson, whose only Court nomination, of Henry Stanbery in1866, was thwarted when the Senate enacted legislation eliminating the Associate Justice position to which Stanbery had been nominated.[5]

As Table 1 shows, the number of nominations made to the Supreme Court has varied greatly from President to President. For any given President, the number of nominations will be affected by various factors, including the length of time the President was in office, the number of vacancies occurring on the Court during that presidency, and whether more than one nomination was required to fill a Court vacancy due to a previous nomination's failure to be confirmed. Examination of the nominations to the Court for each President reveals that half of the 42 Presidents made four or more nominations, and half made three or fewer. Half of the 42 Presidents saw three or more of their Court nominations confirmed, and half saw two or fewer confirmed.

The President with the most Supreme Court nominations and confirmations was George Washington with 14 nominations, 12 of which were confirmed. The two Presidents with the second-largest number of Court nominations were John Tyler and Franklin D. Roosevelt, with nine each. Only one of Tyler's nine nominations, however, received Senate confirmation, while all nine of FDR's were confirmed. The President with the largest number of Supreme Court confirmations in one term (apart from the first eight of George Washington's nominations — all in his first term, and all confirmed) was William Howard Taft, who, during his four years in office, made six Court nominations, all of which were confirmed. Six Presidents made only one Supreme Court nomination each, with the nominations of five of these Presidents receiving confirmation.[6] And, as noted above, three of the nation's 42 Presidents were unable to make a single nomination to the Court, because no vacancies occurred on the Court during their presidencies.

Date That Nominations Were Received in Senate

The Supreme Court appointment process officially begins when the President signs a message to the Senate nominating someone for appointment to the Court. Usually on the date of the signing, the message is delivered to the Senate and recorded in the *Senate Executive Journal* as having been received that day.[7] However, in 30 instances (all but two prior to the 20th century), Supreme Court messages were recorded in the *Senate Executive Journal* as received in the Senate on a day after they were signed by the President — usually the next day. In Table 1, in the "Date received in Senate" column, a second date is provided in parentheses (as the "Nom. date"), whenever a President made a nomination on a day prior to its receipt by the Senate.

Referral of Nominations to Senate Judiciary Committee

Although referral of Supreme Court nominations to the Senate Judiciary Committee is now standard practice, such referrals were not always the case. Table 1 shows that 114 of 158 Supreme Court nominations have been referred to a Senate committee, 113 of them to the Judiciary Committee.

The first standing legislative committees of the Senate, including the Judiciary Committee, were created in 1816. Only once previously was a Supreme Court nomination referred to committee, when, in 1811, the Senate referred the nomination of Alexander Wolcott to a select committee of three Members. For roughly half a century afer the Judiciary Committee's creation, nominations, rather than being automatically referred to the committee, were referred by motion only. From 1816 to 1868, more than two-thirds of the nominations (26 out of 38 nominations), were referred to the committee. During this period, the confirmation success rate was roughly the same for nominations referred, 15 of 26, as it was for those not referred, seven out of 12.

In 1868, Senate rules were changed to provide that all nominations be referred to appropriate standing committees, unless otherwise ordered by the Senate.[8] Subsequently, from 1868 to the present day, 87 of 94 Supreme Court nominations have been referred to the Judiciary Committee. The seven not referred to committee were persons who, at the time of their nomination, were a former President, a Senator, a former Senator, an Attorney General and former U.S. Representative, or a former Secretary of War,[9] and all were easily confirmed. The last Supreme Court nomination not referred to the Judiciary Committee was that of Senator James F.

Byrnes in 1941. The Senate by unanimous consent considered and confirmed the Byrnes nomination, without referral to committee, on the day it received the nomination from the President.

Nominations That Received Public Confirmation Hearings

Table 1, in the "Public hearing date(s)" column, lists dates on which the full Judiciary Committee, or a Judiciary subcommittee, held public confirmation hearings on Supreme Court nominations. Included in this listing are public sessions of the committee at which either Supreme Court nominees testified on their own behalf and/or outside witnesses testified for or against the nominees.

Advent of Public Hearings

Before 1916, the Judiciary Committee considered Supreme Court nominations behind closed doors. Thus, until that year, there are no entries in the "Public hearing date(s)" column. Rather, committee sessions on Court nominations typically were limited to committee members discussing and voting on a nominee in executive session, without hearing testimony from outside witnesses.[10] In 1916, for the first time, the committee held open confirmation hearings on a Supreme Court nomination — that of Louis D. Brandeis to be an Associate Justice — at which outside witnesses (but not the nominee) testified. More days of public hearings (19) were held on the Brandeis nomination than on any Supreme Court nomination since. The Brandeis hearings, however, did not set immediately into place a new policy of open confirmation hearings for Supreme Court nominations, since each of the next six nominations (during the years 1916 to1923) was either considered directly by the Senate, without referral to the Judiciary Committee, or was acted on by the committee without the holding of confirmation hearings.

From 1925 to 1945, public confirmation hearings for Supreme Court nominations became the more common, if not invariable, practice of the Judiciary Committee. In 1925, Harlan F. Stone became the first Supreme Court nominee to appear in person and testify at his confirmation hearings.[11] During the next two decades, the Stone nomination was one of nine Court nominations that received public confirmation hearings before either the full Judiciary Committee or a Judiciary subcommittee,[12] while six other nominations did not receive public hearings. One of the six nominees not receiving a public confirmation hearing was Senator James F. Byrnes, whose nomination in 1941, as noted earlier, was considered directly by the Senate without referral to the Judiciary Committee.[13]

Not indicated in the "Public hearing date(s)"column is the length (in minutes or hours) of each public hearing session. The hearing sessions for a few Supreme Court nominations during the 1925 to1945 period lasted for hours; others, however, were brief and perfunctory in nature, held only long enough to accommodate the small number of witnesses who wished to testify against a nominee.[14]

From Fred M. Vinson's Chief Justice appointment in 1946 through the nomination of Harriet E. Miers to be Associate Justice in 2005, all but three of 34 Supreme Court nominations have received public confirmation hearings before the Senate Judiciary Committee or a Judiciary subcommittee.[15] The first of the three exceptions involved the 1954 nomination of John M. Harlan II, made less than a month before the final adjournment of a Congress. At the beginning of the next Congress, however, Harlan was re-nominated, and hearings were held on that nomination.[16] The second and third exceptions involved the Associate Justice nominations of John G. Roberts Jr. and Harriet E. Miers in 2005, both of which were withdrawn by the President before the scheduled start of confirmation hearings.

Length of Hearings in Days

The number of days given to confirmation hearings has varied greatly from one Supreme Court nomination to another, particularly in recent decades. Following the 19 days of hearings held on the Brandeis nomination in 1916, Court nominations through the Associate Justice nomination of Abe Fortas in 1965 typically received either one or two days of hearings. However, from 1967 through November 2005, 14 of the 20 Court nominations which advanced through the hearings stage received four or more days of open confirmation hearings. Four of the 14 nominations received 11 or more days of hearings,[17] while another received eight days of hearings.[18] By contrast, only three of the 20 nominations received two or fewer days of hearings.[19]

Hearings on the pending nomination of Samuel A. Alito Jr. for Associate Justice are scheduled to begin on January 9, 2006, and are expected to last at least four days.

Nominations Reported Out of Committee to Full Senate

Supreme Court nominations referred to the Judiciary Committee have almost always been reported to the Senate. If a majority of its members oppose confirmation, the Judiciary Committee technically may decide not to report a

Supreme Court nomination. (This tactic would prevent the full Senate from considering the nominee, unless the Senate were able to undertake successfully the discharge of the committee.) Table 1, however, shows that the committee has almost never employed the strategy of not reporting. Of the 113 Supreme Court nominations referred to the Judiciary Committee, it has reported 105 to the Senate.[20] (The pending Alito nomination would be the 106th reported nomination, if the committee ultimately took that action.) The committee has reported these nominations in the following four ways.

Reporting

For most of the first five decades in which the Judiciary Committee considered Supreme Court nominations (1828 to 1863), its usual practice was simply to report these nominations to the Senate, without any official indication of the committee members' opinions regarding them. Twenty-three nominations were reported to the Senate in this way, and 15 of them were confirmed.

Reporting with a Favorable Recommendation

In 1870, the Judiciary Committee initiated the practice of reporting to the Senate an explicit recommendation in favor of confirmation whenever a majority of members supported a Supreme Court nominee. Over the course of almost a century and a half, the committee has favorably reported 71 Supreme Court nominations, with 65 receiving Senate confirmation.[21]

Reporting Without Recommendation

On four occasions — three times in the late 19th century and once in the late 20th century — the Judiciary Committee has voted to report a Supreme Court nomination while explicitly stating it was not making a recommendation to the Senate. On each occasion, the committee reported a nomination without urging the Senate either to confirm or to reject.[22] The Senate confirmed three of the nominations that were reported in this way, while rejecting the fourth.[23]

Reporting with an Unfavorable Recommendation

On seven occasions — five times in the 19th century and twice in the 20th century — the Judiciary Committee voted to report a Supreme Court nomination with a recommendation to the Senate that it reject the nomination. Only two of the seven nominations received Senate confirmation (and each only by a close roll call vote);[24] the Senate rejected four of the others[25] and postponed taking action on the fifth.[26]

Nominations Not Reported Out of Committee

Of the 113 Supreme Court nominations referred to the Judiciary Committee since its establishment, eight were not reported by the committee to the Senate. The final outcome for all eight nominees, however, was determined not by the failure of their nominations to be reported out of committee, but by action, or lack of action, taken outside the committee — by the Senate, Congress as a whole, or the President. While five of the nominees were never confirmed to the Court,[27] the other three ultimately were, after being re-nominated.[28]

Final Action by the Senate or the President

From the first Supreme Court appointments in 1789 to the present day, Presidents have made 157 nominations to the court, not including the pending nomination of Samuel A. Alito Jr. Table 1 shows, in the "Final action by Senate or President" column, that the Senate confirmed 121 of these nominations, or roughly three-fourths.[29] Of the 36 nominations that were not confirmed, 11 were rejected by the Senate (all in roll-call votes),[30] 11 were withdrawn by the President,[31] and 14 lapsed at the end of a session of Congress without a Senate vote cast on whether to confirm.[32]

While the invariable practice of the Senate in recent decades has been to vote on Supreme Court nominations by roll call, this historically was usually not the case. Table 2, at the end of this report, shows that of the132 Senate votes on whether to confirm (resulting in 121 confirmations and 11 rejections), 59 decisions were reached by roll-call votes, and the other 73 by voice vote or unanimous consent.

Initially, for some 40 years, the Senate rarely used roll-call votes to decide Supreme Court nominations. Starting in the 1830s, however, and continuing through the 1880s, the Senate used roll-call votes on Supreme Court nominations somewhat more often than unrecorded votes. The trend reversed between 1890 and 1965, when fewer than one-third of Senate decisions on confirming Court nominations were by roll-call vote. Since 1967, though, every Senate vote on whether to confirm a Supreme Court nomination has been by roll call. Table 2 shows these trends within the four historical periods just noted, by breaking down the number of Senate decisions on confirmation within each period according to whether made by voice vote or unanimous consent (UC) on the one hand, or by roll-call vote, on the other. As already mentioned, all 11 Senate rejections of Supreme Court nominations were accomplished by roll-call votes.

Historically, recorded vote margins on Supreme Court nominations have varied considerably. Some roll-call votes, either confirming or rejecting a nomination, have been close.[33] Most votes, however, have been overwhelmingly in favor of confirmation.[34]

Days from Date of Senate Receipt of Nomination to First Hearing

For Supreme Court nominations, the amount of time elapsing between Senate receipt and start of confirmation hearings has varied greatly. Table 1 shows that, for all 41 Court nominations receiving public confirmation hearings (starting with the Brandeis nomination in 1916), the shortest time that elapsed between Senate receipt and start of hearings was two days, for the nomination of Felix Frankfurter in 1939; the second-shortest time interval of this sort was four days, also in 1939, for the nomination of William O. Douglas. The longest time elapsing between Senate receipt and first day of confirmation hearings was 82 days, for the nomination of Potter Stewart in 1959; the next-longest time interval of this sort was 70 days, for nominee Robert H. Bork in 1987.

In recent decades, from the late 1960s to the present, the Judiciary Committee has tended to take more time in starting hearings on Supreme Court nominations than it did previously. Table 1 reveals that prior to 1967, a median of 11 days elapsed between Senate receipt of Supreme Court nominations and the first day of confirmation hearings. From the Supreme Court nomination of Thurgood Marshall in 1967 through the nomination of John G. Roberts Jr. to be Chief Justice in 2005,[35] a median of 15 days elapsed between Senate receipt and first day of confirmation hearings.[36]

Starting in the 1990s, the inclination of the Judiciary Committee has been to allow at least four weeks to pass between Senate receipt of Supreme Court nominations and the start of confirmation hearings. This block of time is intended to be used by the committee members and staff for thorough study and review of background information about nominees and issues relevant to their nominations, in preparation for the hearings. In the case of four of the five most recent Court nominations to receive confirmation hearings (starting with the David H. Souter nomination in 1990), the shortest elapsed time between Senate receipt and first day of hearings was 28 days.[37] While the elapsed time for the fifth nomination, of John G. Roberts Jr. to be Chief Justice in 2005, was only six days, another, longer time interval is more meaningful. Table 1 shows that Roberts's earlier nomination to be Associate Justice — later withdrawn, in order to have Roberts be re-nominated for Chief Justice — was received by the Senate 45 days prior to the start of hearings on his Chief Justice nomination. Confirmation hearings on the pending Supreme Court nomination of Samuel A. Alito Jr. are scheduled to begin on January 9, 2006, 60 days after Senate receipt of the nomination on November 10, 2005.

Days from Senate Receipt to Final Committee Vote

The time elapsing between Senate receipt of Supreme Court nominations from the President and final committee votes has also varied greatly. Table 1 shows that, for the 107 Court nominations that received final committee votes,[38] the nomination receiving the most prompt committee vote was of Caleb Cushing in 1874, which was reported by the Judiciary Committee on the same day that the Senate received it from the President.[39] The committee votes on 14 other nominations to the court occurred three days or less after the dates of Senate receipt.[40] At the other extreme was the 1916 nomination of Louis D. Brandeis, on which the Judiciary Committee voted 117 days after Senate receipt and referral to the committee. Five other nominations as well, one in the 19th century and four in the 20th, received committee votes more than 80 days after Senate receipt from the President.[41]

In recent decades, the Judiciary Committee has taken much more time in casting a final vote on Supreme Court nominations than it did previously. Table 1 shows that prior to 1967, a median of nine days elapsed between Senate receipt of Supreme Court nominations and the committee's final vote on reporting them to the full Senate.[42] From the Supreme Court nomination of Thurgood Marshall in 1967 through the nomination of John G. Roberts Jr. to be Chief Justice in 2005, a median of 37 days elapsed between Senate receipt and final committee vote.[43]

Somewhat earlier, during the presidency of Dwight Eisenhower (1953 to 1961), four Supreme Court nominations all were pending, prior to Judiciary Committee vote, well in excess of the 1967 to 2005 median of 37 days for that time interval;[44] however, the corresponding time intervals for the next three Court nominations (two by President John F. Kennedy and one by President Lyndon B. Johnson) were all well below the 37-day median.[45]

Days from Senate Receipt to Final Senate or Presidential Action

The Supreme Court confirmation process now typically extends over a much longer period of time than it once did. Table 1 shows that from the appointment of the first Justices in 1789, continuing into the early 20th century, most Senate confirmations of Supreme Court nominees occurred within a week of the nominations being made by the President. In recent decades, by contrast, it has become the norm for the Court appointment process — from Senate receipt of nominations from the President to Senate confirmation or other final action (such as Senate rejection, or withdrawal by the President) — to take more than two months.

The last column of Table 1 shows the number of days that elapsed from the dates Supreme Court nominations were received in the Senate until the dates of final Senate or presidential action. The number of elapsed days is shown for 149 of the 158 nominations listed in the table, with no elapsed time shown for the pending Alito nomination or for eight nominations on which there was no record of any kind of official or effective final action by the Senate or by the President.[46] At the bottom of the table, the median number of elapsed days from initial Senate receipt until final action by the Senate or the President is shown for three historical periods — 1789-2005, 1789-1966, and 1967-2005.

In recent decades, the median elapsed time for Supreme Court nominations to receive final action has increased dramatically, dwarfing the median time taken on earlier nominations. Table 1 shows that from 1967 (starting with the nomination of Thurgood Marshall) through 2005 (ending with the nomination of John G. Roberts Jr. for Chief Justice), a median of 67 days elapsed from when a Supreme Court nomination was received in the Senate until the date it received final action, compared with a median of seven days for the same interval for the prior years of 1789 to 1966.[47] Most of the Supreme Court nominations receiving final action within a relatively brief period of time — for example, within three days of initial receipt in the Senate —occurred before the 20th century,[48] while most of the nominations receiving final action after a relatively long period of time — for example, 75 days or more after receipt in the Senate — occurred in the 20th century (and nearly all of these since 1967).[49]

The presence of Senate committee involvement has clearly tended to increase the overall length of the Supreme Court confirmation process. Of the 26 Court nominations made prior to the establishment of the Judiciary Committee in 1816, only one, of Alexander Wolcott in 1811, received final action more than seven days after initial Senate receipt (being rejected by the Senate nine days after receipt). It also was the only Court nomination prior to 1816 which was referred to, and considered by, a select committee. Subsequently, until the Civil War, six nominations received final action more than 50 days after initial Senate receipt. All six were first considered and reported by the Judiciary Committee. During the same period, other Court nominations were considered and acted on by the Senate more quickly – some with, and some without, first being referred to committee.

Subsequent historical developments involving the Senate Judiciary Committee further served to increase the median length of the Supreme Court confirmation process. One such development was the Senate's adoption of a rule in 1868 that nominations be referred to appropriate standing committees, resulting in the referral of nearly all Supreme Court nominations thereafter to the Judiciary Committee. Another was the increasing practice of the Judiciary Committee in the 20th century of holding public confirmation hearings on Supreme Court nominations (ultimately to become standard practice). A third, more recent, historical trend has involved the pace and thoroughness of the Judiciary Committee in preparing for and conducting confirmation hearings. Since the late 1960s, close and thorough examination of the background, qualifications, and views of Supreme Court nominees has become the norm for the Judiciary Committee, an approach that typically extends the confirmation process by at least several weeks, as a result of preparation for and holding of confirmation hearings.

Recess Appointments to the Supreme Court

On 12 occasions in the nation's history, Presidents have made temporary recess appointments to the Supreme Court without submitting nominations to the Senate. Table 1 identifies all of these 12 appointments, showing how each was related to a later nomination of the appointee for the same position. The table shows that nine of the 12 recess appointments were made before the end of the Civil War,[50] with the last three made almost a century later, in the 1950s, during the presidency of Dwight D. Eisenhower.[51]

Each of the 12 recess appointments occurred when a President exercised his power under the Constitution to make recess appointments when the Senate was not in session.[52] Historically, when recesses between sessions of the Senate were much longer than they are today, recess appointments served the purpose of averting long vacancies on the Court when the Senate was unavailable to confirm a President's appointees. The terms of these recess appointments, however, were limited by the constitutional requirement that they expire at the end of the next session of Congress (unlike the lifetime appointments Court appointees receive when nominated and then confirmed by the Senate).[53]

Despite the temporary nature of these appointments, every person appointed during a recess of the Senate except for one — John Rutledge, to be Chief Justice, in 1795 — ultimately received a lifetime appointment to the Court after being nominated by the President and confirmed by the Senate. As Table 1 shows, all 12 of the recess appointees were subsequently nominated to the same position, and 11 (all except for Rutledge) were confirmed.

CONCLUDING OBSERVATIONS

The preceding discussion suggests that Senate treatment of Supreme Court nominations has gone through various phases during the more than 200 years of the Republic. Initially, such nominations were handled without Senate committee involvement. Later, from 1816 to 1868, most nominations to the Supreme Court were referred to the Judiciary Committee, but only by motion. Since 1868, as the result of a change in its rules, the Senate has referred nearly all Court nominations to the Judiciary Committee. During the rest of the 19th century and early 20th century, the committee considered nominations without public hearings. Subsequently, public hearings gradually became the more common, if not invariable, committee practice, although many of the earlier hearings were perfunctory and held simply to accommodate a small number of witnesses wishing to testify against the nominees. Gradually, however, in the latter half of the 20th century, public hearings on Supreme Court nominations lasting four or more days, with nominees present to answer extensive questioning from committee members, would become the usual practice.

Also, the overall length of time taken by the Supreme Court confirmation process has, in general, increased significantly over the course of more than 200 years. From the appointment of the first Justices in 1789, continuing well into the 20th century, most Supreme Court nominations received final action (usually, but not always, in the form of Senate confirmation) within a week of being submitted by the President to the Senate. In recent decades, by contrast, it has become the norm for the confirmation process to take from two to three months.

Other trends and historical phases may be discerned from Tables 1 and 2. Still other trends, of course, may be revealed by future nominations that Presidents make and by the actions taken on them by the Senate and its Judiciary Committee.

Table 1. Nominations to the Supreme Court of the United States, 1789-2005

Nominee	President	Date received in Senate [a]	Senate committee actions			Final action by Senate or President		Days from date received in Senate to:		
			Public hearing date(s)	Final vote date [b]	Final vote	Date	Final action [c]	First hearing date	Committee final vote date	Final action by Senate or President
John Jay of New York (Chief Justice – hereafter C. J.)	Washington	09/24/1789	Nomination predated creation of Judiciary Committee in 12/10/1816. No record of other committee referral.			09/26/1789	Confirmed	—	—	2
John Rutledge of South Carolina	Washington	09/24/1789				09/26/1789	Confirmed	—	—	2
William Cushing of Massachusetts	Washington	09/24/1789				09/26/1789	Confirmed	—	—	2
Robert Harrison of Maryland	Washington	09/24/1789				09/26/1789	Confirmed (Nominee declined)	—	—	2
James Wilson of Pennsylvania	Washington	09/24/1789				09/26/1789	Confirmed	—	—	2
John Blair Jr. of Virginia	Washington	09/24/1789				09/26/1789	Confirmed	—	—	2
James Iredell of North Carolina	Washington	02/09/1790 (Nom. date 02/08/1790)				02/10/1790	Confirmed	—	—	1
Thomas Johnson of Maryland	Washington	*Recess Appointment, 08/05/1791*								
		11/01/1791 (Nom. date 10/31/1791)	Nomination predated creation of Judiciary Committee in 12/10/1816. No record of other committee referral.			11/07/1791	Confirmed	—	—	6
William Paterson of New Jersey	Washington	02/27/1793				02/28/1793	Withdrawn	—	—	1

Table 1. Nominations to the Supreme Court of the United States, 1789-2005 (Continued)

Nominee	President	Date received in Senate [a]	Senate committee actions			Final action by Senate or President		Days from date received in Senate to:		
			Public hearing date(s)	Final vote date [b]	Final vote	Date	Final action [c]	First hearing date	Committee final vote date	Final action by Senate or President
William Paterson of New Jersey	Washington	03/04/1793				03/04/1793	Confirmed	—	—	0
John Rutledge of South Carolina (C. J.)	Washington	*Recess Appointment, 07/01/1795*								
		12/10/1795	Nomination predated creation of Judiciary Committee in 12/10/1816. No record of other committee referral.			12/15/1795	Rejected (10-14)	—	—	5
William Cushing of Massachusetts (C. J.)	Washington	01/26/1796				01/27/1796	Confirmed (Nominee declined)	—	—	1
Samuel Chase of Maryland	Washington	01/26/1796				01/27/1796	Confirmed	—	—	1
Oliver Ellsworth of Connecticut (C. J.)	Washington	03/03/1796				03/04/1796	Confirmed (21-1)	—	—	1
Bushrod Washington of Virginia	J. Adams	*Recess Appointment, 09/29/1798*								
		12/19/1798	Nomination predated creation of Judiciary Committee in 12/10/1816. No record of other committee referral.			12/20/1798	Confirmed	—	—	1
Alfred Moore of North Carolina	J. Adams	12/04/1799				12/10/1799	Confirmed	—	—	6
John Jay of New York (C. J.)	J. Adams	12/18/1800				12/19/1800	Confirmed (Nominee declined)	—	—	1
John Marshall of Virginia (C. J.)	J. Adams	01/20/1801				01/27/1801	Confirmed	—	—	7
William Johnson of South Carolina	Jefferson	03/22/1804				03/24/1804	Confirmed	—	—	2

Table 1. Nominations to the Supreme Court of the United States, 1789-2005 (Continued)

Nominee	President	Date received in Senate [a]	Senate committee actions			Final action by Senate or President		Days from date received in Senate to:		
			Public hearing date(s)	Final vote date [b]	Final vote	Date	Final action [c]	First hearing date	Committee final vote date	Final action by Senate or President
H. Brockholst Livingston of New York	Jefferson	*Recess Appointment, 11/10/1806*								
		12/15/1806	Nomination predated creation of Judiciary Committee in 12/10/1816. No record of other committee referral.			12/17/1806	Confirmed	—	—	2
Thomas Todd of Kentucky	Jefferson	02/28/1807				03/02/1807	Confirmed	—	—	2
Levi Lincoln of Massachusetts	Madison	01/02/1811				01/03/1811	Confirmed (Nominee declined)	—	—	1
Alexander Wolcott of Connecticut	Madison	02/04/1811	No record of hearing	Select Committee, 02/13/1811	Reported	02/13/1811	Rejected (9-24)	—	9	9
John Quincy Adams of Massachusetts	Madison	02/21/1811	Nomination predated creation of Judiciary Committee in 12/10/1816. No record of other committee referral.			02/22/1811	Confirmed (Nominee declined)	—	—	1
Joseph Story of Massachusetts	Madison	11/15/1811				11/18/1811	Confirmed	—	—	3
Gabriel Duvall of Maryland	Madison	11/15/1811				11/18/1811	Confirmed	—	—	3
Smith Thompson of New York	Monroe	*Recess Appointment, 09/01/1823*								
		12/08/1823 (Nom. date 12/5/1823)	Nomination was not referred to Judiciary Committee.			12/09/1823	Confirmed	—	—	1
Robert Trimble of Kentucky	J. Q. Adams	04/12/1826 (Nom. date 04/11/1826)	Motion to refer to Judiciary Committee rejected by Senate, 05/09/1826 (7-25)			05/09/1826	Confirmed (27-5)	—	—	27

Table 1. Nominations to the Supreme Court of the United States, 1789-2005 (Continued)

Nominee	President	Date received in Senate [a]	Senate committee actions			Final action by Senate or President		Days from date received in Senate to:		
			Public hearing date(s)	Final vote date [b]	Final vote	Date	Final action [c]	First hearing date	Committee final vote date	Final action by Senate or President
John Crittenden of Kentucky	J. Q. Adams	12/18/1828 (Nom. date 12/17/1828)	No record of hearing	01/26/1829	Reported with recommendation not to act	02/12/1829	Postponed (23-17)	—	39	56
John McLean of Ohio	Jackson	03/06/1829	Nomination was not referred to Judiciary Committee.			03/07/1829	Confirmed	—	—	1
Henry Baldwin of Pennsylvania	Jackson	01/05/1830	Nomination was not referred to Judiciary Committee.			01/05/1830	Confirmed (41-2)	—	—	0
James M. Wayne of Georgia	Jackson	01/07/1835 (Nom. date 01/06/1835)	No record of hearing	01/09/1835	Reported	01/09/1835	Confirmed	—	2	2
Roger B. Taney of Maryland	Jackson	01/15/1835	Nomination was not referred to Judiciary Committee.			03/03/1835	Postponed (24-21)	—	—	47
Roger B. Taney of Maryland (C. J.)	Jackson	12/28/1835	No record of hearing	01/05/1836	Reported	Motion to proceed, 03/14/1836 (25-19)		—	8	78
						03/15/1836	Confirmed (29-15)			
Philip P. Barbour of Virginia	Jackson	12/28/1835	No record of hearing	01/05/1836	Reported	Motion to proceed, 03/15/1836 (25-20)		—	8	78
						03/15/1836	Confirmed (30-11)			

Table 1. Nominations to the Supreme Court of the United States, 1789-2005 (Continued)

Nominee	President	Date received in Senate [a]	Senate committee actions			Final action by Senate or President		Days from date received in Senate to:		
			Public hearing date(s)	Final vote date [b]	Final vote	Date	Final action [c]	First hearing date	Committee final vote date	Final action by Senate or President
William Smith of Alabama	Jackson	03/03/1837	No record of hearing	03/08/1837	Reported	03/08/1837	Confirmed (23-18) (Nominee declined)	—	5	5
John Catron of Tennessee	Jackson	03/03/1837	No record of hearing	03/08/1837	Reported	03/08/1837	Confirmed (28-15)	—	5	5
John McKinley of Alabama	Van Buren	*Recess Appointment, 04/22/1837*								
		09/19/1837 (Nom. date 09/18/1837)	No record of hearing	09/25/1837	Reported	09/25/1837	Confirmed	—	6	6
Peter V. Daniel of Virginia	Van Buren	02/27/1841 (Nom. date 02/25/1841)	Nomination was not referred to Judiciary Committee.			03/02/1841	Confirmed (22-5)	—	—	3
John C. Spencer of New York	Tyler	01/09/1844 (Nom. date 01/08/1844	No record of hearing	01/30/1844	Reported	01/31/1844	Rejected (21-26)	—	21	22
Reuben H. Walworth of New York	Tyler	03/13/1844	No record of hearing	06/14/1844	Reported	Tabled, 06/15/1844 (27-20)		—	93	96
						06/17/1844	Withdrawn			
Edward King of Pennsylvania	Tyler	06/05/1844	No record of hearing	06/14/1844	Reported	06/15/1844	Tabled (29-18)	—	9	10
John C. Spencer of New York	Tyler	06/17/1844	Nomination was not referred to Judiciary Committee.			06/17/1844	Withdrawn	—	—	0

Table 1. Nominations to the Supreme Court of the United States, 1789-2005 (Continued)

Nominee	President	Date received in Senate [a]	Senate committee actions			Final action by Senate or President		Days from date received in Senate to:		
			Public hearing date(s)	Final vote date [b]	Final vote	Date	Final action [c]	First hearing date	Committee final vote date	Final action by Senate or President
Reuben H. Walworth of New York	Tyler	06/17/1844	Nomination was not referred to Judiciary Committee.			No record of action		—	—	—
Reuben H. Walworth of New York	Tyler	12/10/1844 (Nom. date 12/04/1844)	No record of hearing	01/21/1845	Reported	Tabled, 01/21/1845		—	42	58
						02/06/1845	Withdrawn			
Edward King of Pennsylvania	Tyler	12/10/1844 (Nom. date 12/04/1844)	No record of hearing	01/21/1845	Reported	Tabled, 01/21/1845		—	42	60
						02/08/1845	Withdrawn			
Samuel Nelson of New York	Tyler	02/06/1845 (Nom. date 02/04/1845)	No record of hearing	02/08/1845	Reported	02/14/1845	Confirmed	—	2	8
John M. Read of Pennsylvania	Tyler	02/08/1845	No record of hearing	02/14/1845	Reported	No record of action		—	6	—
George W. Woodward of Pennsylvania	Polk	12/23/1845	No record of hearing	01/20/1846	Reported	Motion to postpone rejected, 01/22/1846 (21-28)		—	28	30
						01/22/1846	Rejected (20-29)			
Levi Woodbury of New Hampshire	Polk	*Recess Appointment, 09/20/1845*								
		12/23/1845	No record of hearing	01/03/1846	Reported	01/03/1846	Confirmed	—	11	11

Table 1. Nominations to the Supreme Court of the United States, 1789-2005 (Continued)

Nominee	President	Date received in Senate [a]	Senate committee actions			Final action by Senate or President		Days from date received in Senate to:		
			Public hearing date(s)	Final vote date [b]	Final vote	Date	Final action [c]	First hearing date	Committee final vote date	Final action by Senate or President
Robert C. Grier of Pennsylvania	Polk	08/03/1846	No record of hearing	08/04/1846	Reported	08/04/1846	Confirmed	—	1	1
Benjamin R. Curtis of Massachusetts	Fillmore	*Recess Appointment, 09/22/1851*								
		12/12/1851 (Nom. date 12/11/1851)	No record of hearing	12/23/1851	Reported	12/23/1851	Confirmed	—	11	11
Edward A. Bradford of Louisiana	Fillmore	08/21/1852 (Nom. date 08/16/1852)	No record of hearing	08/30/1852	Reported	08/31/1852	Tabled	—	9	10
George E. Badger of North Carolina	Fillmore	01/10/1853 (Nom. date 01/03/1853)	Nomination was not referred to Judiciary Committee.			02/11/1853	Postponed (26-25)	—	—	32
William C. Micou of Louisiana	Fillmore	02/24/1853 (Nom. date 02/14/1853)	No record of hearing	Referred to Judiciary Committee on 02/24/1853. Senate ordered committee discharged of nomination on same day; no record of Senate consideration after discharge.				—	—	—
John A. Campbell of Alabama	Pierce	03/21/1853	No record of hearing	03/22/1853	Reported	03/22/1853	Confirmed	—	1	1
Nathan Clifford of Maine	Buchanan	12/09/1857	No record of hearing	01/06/1858	Reported	01/12/1858	Confirmed (26-23)	—	28	34

Table 1. Nominations to the Supreme Court of the United States, 1789-2005 (Continued)

Nominee	President	Date received in Senate [a]	Senate committee actions			Final action by Senate or President		Days from date received in Senate to:		
			Public hearing date(s)	Final vote date [b]	Final vote	Date	Final action [c]	First hearing date	Committee final vote date	Final action by Senate or President
Jeremiah S. Black of Pennsylvania	Buchanan	02/06/1861 (Nom. date 02/05/1861)	Nomination was not referred to Judiciary Committee.			02/21/1861	Motion to proceed rejected (25-26)	—	—	15
Noah H. Swayne of Ohio	Lincoln	01/22/1862 (Nom. date 01/21/1862)	No record of hearing	01/24/1862	Reported	01/24/1862	Confirmed (38-1)	—	2	2
Samuel F. Miller of Iowa	Lincoln	07/16/1862	Nomination was not referred to Judiciary Committee.			07/16/1862	Confirmed	—	—	0
David Davis of Illinois	Lincoln	*Recess Appointment, 10/17/1862*								
		12/03/1862 (Nom. date 12/01/1862)	No record of hearing	12/05/1862	Reported	12/08/1862	Confirmed	—	2	5
Stephen J. Field of California	Lincoln	03/07/1863 (Nom. date 03/06/1863	No record of hearing	03/09/1863	Reported	03/10/1863	Confirmed	—	2	3
Salmon P. Chase of Ohio (C. J.)	Lincoln	12/06/1864	Nomination was not referred to Judiciary Committee.			12/06/1864	Confirmed	—	—	0
Henry Stanbery of Ohio	A. Johnson	04/16/1866	No record of hearing	Referred to Judiciary Committee on 04/16/1866. No record of committee vote, and no record of Senate action after referral.				—	—	—
Ebenezer R. Hoar of Massachusetts	Grant	12/15/1869 (Nom. date 12/14/1869)	No record of hearing	12/22/1869	Reported adversely	02/03/1870	Rejected (24-33)	—	7	50

Table 1. Nominations to the Supreme Court of the United States, 1789-2005 (Continued)

Nominee	President	Date received in Senate [a]	Senate committee actions			Final action by Senate or President		Days from date received in Senate to:		
			Public hearing date(s)	Final vote date [b]	Final vote	Date	Final action [c]	First hearing date	Committee final vote date	Final action by Senate or President
Edwin M. Stanton of Pennsylvania	Grant	12/20/1869	Nomination was not referred to Judiciary Committee			12/20/1869	Confirmed (46-11)	—	—	0
William Strong of Pennsylvania	Grant	02/08/1870 (Nom. date 02/07/1870)	No record of hearing	02/14/1870	Reported favorably	02/18/1870	Confirmed	—	6	10
Joseph P. Bradley of New Jeresy	Grant	02/08/1870 (Nom. date 02/07/1870)	No record of hearing	02/14/1870	Reported favorably	Postponed, 03/02/1870 (31-26)			—	6 41
Ward Hunt of New York	Grant	12/06/1872 (Nom. date 12/03/1872)	No record of hearing	12/11/1872	Reported favorably	12/11/1872	Confirmed	—	5	5
George H. Williams of Oregon (C. J.)	Grant	12/02/1873 (Nom. date 12/01/1873)	No record of hearing	12/11/1873	Reported favorably	Recommitted, 12/15/1873		—	9	37
			Closed hearings [d] 12/16/1873 12/17/1873	—		01/08/1874	Withdrawn			
Caleb Cushing of Massachusetts (C. J.)	Grant	01/09/1874	No record of hearing	01/09/1874	Reported favorably	01/14/1874	Withdrawn	—	0	5
Morrison R. Waite of Ohio (C. J.)	Grant	01/19/1874	No record of hearing	01/20/1874	Reported favorably	01/21/1874	Confirmed (63-0)	—	1	2
John Marshall Harlan of Kentucky	Hayes	10/17/1877	No record of hearing	11/26/1877	Reported favorably	11/29/1877	Confirmed	—	40	43

Table 1. Nominations to the Supreme Court of the United States, 1789-2005 (Continued)

Nominee	President	Date received in Senate [a]	Senate committee actions			Final action by Senate or President		Days from date received in Senate to:		
			Public hearing date(s)	Final vote date [b]	Final vote	Date	Final action [c]	First hearing date	Committee final vote date	Final action by Senate or President
William B. Woods of Georgia	Hayes	12/15/1880	No record of hearing	12/20/1880	Reported favorably	12/21/1880	Confirmed (39-8)	—	5	6
						Tabled motion to reconsider, 12/22/1880 (36-3)				
Stanley Matthews of Ohio	Hayes	01/26/1881	No record of hearing	Considered on 02/07/1881		No record of action		—	19	—
				02/14/1881	Postponed					
Stanley Matthews of Ohio	Garfield	03/18/1881 (Nom. date 03/14/1881)	No record of hearing	05/09/1881	Reported adversely (6-1)	05/12/1881	Confirmed (24-23)	—	53	55
Horace Gray of Massachusetts	Arthur	12/19/1881	No record of hearing	12/20/1881	Reported favorably	12/20/1881	Confirmed (51-5)	—	1	1
Roscoe Conkling of New York	Arthur	02/24/1882	No record of hearing	03/02/1882	Reported favorably	03/02/1882	Confirmed (39-12) (Nominee declined)	—	6	6
Samuel Blatchford of New York	Arthur	03/13/1882	No record of hearing	03/22/1882	Reported favorably	03/22/1882	Confirmed	—	9	9
Lucius Q. C. Lamar of Mississippi	Cleveland	12/12/1887 (Nom. date 12/06/1887)	No record of hearing	01/10/1888	Reported adversely	01/16/1888	Confirmed (32-28)	—	29	35

Table 1. Nominations to the Supreme Court of the United States, 1789-2005 (Continued)

Nominee	President	Date received in Senate [a]	Senate committee actions			Final action by Senate or President		Days from date received in Senate to:		
			Public hearing date(s)	Final vote date [b]	Final vote	Date	Final action [c]	First hearing date	Committee final vote date	Final action by Senate or President
Melville W. Fuller of Illinois (C. J.)	Cleveland	05/02/1888 (Nom. date 04/30/1888)	No record of hearing	07/02/1888	Reported without recommendation	07/20/1888	Confirmed (41-20)	—	61	79
David J. Brewer of Kansas	Harrison	12/04/1889	No record of hearing	12/16/1889	Reported favorably	Motion to postpone rejected, 12/18/1889 (15-54)		—	12	14
						Motion to postpone rejected, 12/18/1889 (25-45)				
						12/18/1889	Confirmed (53-11)			
Henry B. Brown of Michigan	Harrison	12/23/1890	No record of hearing	12/29/1890	Reported favorably	12/29/1890	Confirmed	—	6	6
George Shiras Jr. of Pennsylvania	Harrison	07/19/1892	No record of hearing	07/25/1892	Reported without recommendation	07/26/1892	Confirmed	—	6	7
Howell E. Jackson of Tennessee	Harrison	02/02/1893	No record of hearing	02/13/1893	Reported favorably	02/18/1893	Confirmed	—	11	16
William B. Hornblower of New York	Cleveland	09/19/1893	No record of hearing	Considered on 09/25/1893 and 10/25/1893		No record of action		—	—	—

Table 1. Nominations to the Supreme Court of the United States, 1789-2005 (Continued)

Nominee	President	Date received in Senate [a]	Senate committee actions			Final action by Senate or President		Days from date received in Senate to:		
			Public hearing date(s)	Final vote date [b]	Final vote	Date	Final action [c]	First hearing date	Committee final vote date	Final action by Senate or President
William B. Hornblower of New York	Cleveland	12/06/1893	No record of hearing	01/08/1894	Reported adversely	01/15/1894	Rejected (24-30)	—	33	40
Wheeler H. Peckham of New York	Cleveland	01/22/1894	No record of hearing	02/12/1894	Reported without recommendation	02/16/1894	Rejected (32-41)	—	21	25
Edward D. White of Louisiana	Cleveland	02/19/1894	Nomination was not referred to Judiciary Committee			02/19/1894	Confirmed	—	—	0
Rufus W. Peckham of New York	Cleveland	12/03/1895	No record of hearing	12/09/1895	Reported favorably	12/09/1895	Confirmed	—	6	6
Joseph McKenna of California	McKinley	12/16/1897	No record of hearing	01/13/1898	Reported favorably	01/21/1898	Confirmed	—	28	36
Oliver Wendell Holmes of Massachusetts	T. Roosevelt	12/02/1902	No record of hearing	12/04/1902	Reported favorably	12/04/1902	Confirmed	—	2	2
William R. Day of Ohio	T. Roosevelt	02/19/1903	No record of hearing	02/23/1903	Reported favorably	02/23/1903	Confirmed	—	4	4

Table 1. Nominations to the Supreme Court of the United States, 1789-2005 (Continued)

Nominee	President	Date received in Senate [a]	Senate committee actions			Final action by Senate or President		Days from date received in Senate to:		
			Public hearing date(s)	Final vote date [b]	Final vote	Date	Final action [c]	First hearing date	Committee final vote date	Final action by Senate or President
William H. Moody of Massachusetts	T. Roosevelt	12/03/1906	No record of hearing	12/10/1906	Reported favorably	12/12/1906	Confirmed	—	7	9
Horace H. Lurton of Tennessee	Taft	12/13/1909	No record of hearing	12/16/1909	Reported favorably	12/20/1909	Confirmed	—	3	7
Charles Evans Hughes of New York	Taft	04/25/1910	No record of hearing	05/02/1910	Reported favorably	05/02/1910	Confirmed	—	7	7
Edward D. White of Louisiana (C. J.)	Taft	12/12/1910	Nomination was not referred to Judiciary Committee.			12/12/1910	Confirmed	—	—	0
Willis Van Devanter of Wyoming	Taft	12/12/1910	No record of hearing	12/15/1910	Reported favorably	12/15/1910	Confirmed	—	3	3
Joseph R. Lamar of Georgia	Taft	12/12/1910	No record of hearing	12/15/1910	Reported favorably	12/15/1910	Confirmed	—	3	3
Mahlon Pitney of New Jersey	Taft	02/19/1912	No record of hearing	03/04/1912	Reported favorably	03/13/1912	Confirmed (50-26)	—	14	23
James C. McReynolds of Tennessee	Wilson	08/19/1914	No record of hearing	08/24/1914	Reported favorably	08/29/1914	Confirmed (44-6)	—	5	10

Table 1. Nominations to the Supreme Court of the United States, 1789-2005 (Continued)

Nominee	President	Date received in Senate [a]	Senate committee actions			Final action by Senate or President		Days from date received in Senate to:		
			Public hearing date(s)	Final vote date [b]	Final vote	Date	Final action [c]	First hearing date	Committee final vote date	Final action by Senate or President
Louis D. Brandeis of Massachusetts	Wilson	01/28/1916	02/09/1916 02/10/1916 02/15/1916 02/16/1916 02/17/1916 02/18/1916 02/24/1916 02/25/1916 02/26/1916 02/29/1916 03/01/1916 03/02/1916 03/03/1916 03/04/1916 03/06/1916 03/07/1916 03/08/1916 03/14/1916 03/15/1916	05/24/1916	Reported favorably (10-8)	06/01/1916	Confirmed (47-22)	12	117	125
John H. Clarke of Ohio	Wilson	07/14/1916	No record of hearing	07/24/1916	Reported favorably	07/24/1916	Confirmed	—	10	10
William Howard Taft of Connecticut (C. J.)	Harding	06/30/1921	Nomination was not referred to Judiciary Committee.			06/30/1921	Confirmed (60-4) [e]	—	—	0
George Sutherland of Utah	Harding	09/05/1922	Nomination was not referred to Judiciary Committee.			09/05/1922	Confirmed	—	—	0
Pierce Butler of Minnesota	Harding	11/23/1922 (Nom. date 11/22/1922)	No record of hearing	11/28/1922	Reported favorably	Placed on the Executive Calendar on 11/28/1922, with no record of further action		—	5	—

Table 1. Nominations to the Supreme Court of the United States, 1789-2005 (Continued)

Nominee	President	Date received in Senate [a]	Senate committee actions			Final action by Senate or President		Days from date received in Senate to:		
			Public hearing date(s)	Final vote date [b]	Final vote	Date	Final action [c]	First hearing date	Committee final vote date	Final action by Senate or President
Pierce Butler of Minnesota	Harding	12/05/1922	No record of hearing	12/18/1922	Reported favorably	Motion to recommit defeated, 12/21/1922 (7-63)		—	13	16
						12/21/1922	Confirmed (61-8)			
Edward T. Sanford of Tennessee	Harding	01/24/1923	No record of hearing	01/29/1923	Reported favorably	01/29/1923	Confirmed	—	5	5
Harlan F. Stone of New York	Coolidge	01/05/1925	Closed hearing 01/12/1925	Reported favorably 01/21/1925		Recommitted 01/26/1925		—	28	31
			01/28/1925 (after 01/26/1925 recomt'l) [f]	02/02/1925	Reported favorably	02/05/1925	Confirmed (71-6)	23		
Charles Evans Hughes of New York (C. J.)	Hoover	02/03/1930	No record of hearing	02/10/1930	Reported favorably (10-2)	Motion to recommit rejected, 02/13/1930 (31-49)			—	7 10
						02/13/1930	Confirmed (52-26)			
John J. Parker of North Carolina	Hoover	03/21/1930	04/05/1930	04/17/1930	Reported adversely (10-6)	05/07/1930	Rejected (39-41)	15	27	47
Owen J. Roberts of Pennsylvania	Hoover	05/09/1930	No record of hearing	05/19/1930	Reported favorably	05/20/1930	Confirmed	—	10	11

Table 1. Nominations to the Supreme Court of the United States, 1789-2005 (Continued)

Nominee	President	Date received in Senate [a]	Senate committee actions			Final action by Senate or President		Days from date received in Senate to:		
			Public hearing date(s)	Final vote date [b]	Final vote	Date	Final action [c]	First hearing date	Committee final vote date	Final action by Senate or President
Benjamin N. Cardozo of New York	Hoover	02/15/1932	02/19/1932	02/23/1932	Reported favorably	02/24/1932	Confirmed	4	8	9
Hugo L. Black of Alabama	F. Roosevelt	08/12/1937	No record of hearing	08/16/1937	Reported favorably (13-4)	Motion to recommit rejected, 08/17/1937 (15-66)			—	4 5
						08/17/1937	Confirmed (63-16)			
Stanley F. Reed of Kentucky	F. Roosevelt	01/15/1938	01/20/1938	01/24/1938	Reported favorably	01/25/1938	Confirmed	5	9	10
Felix Frankfurter of Massachusetts	F. Roosevelt	01/05/1939	01/07/1939 01/10/1939 01/11/1939 01/12/1939	01/16/1939	Reported favorably	01/17/1939	Confirmed	2	11	12
William O. Douglas of Connecticut	F. Roosevelt	03/20/1939	03/24/1939	03/27/1939	Reported favorably	04/04/1939	Confirmed (62-4)	4	7	15
Frank Murphy of Michigan	F. Roosevelt	01/04/1940	No record of hearing	01/15/1940	Reported favorably	01/16/1940	Confirmed	—	11	12
Harlan F. Stone of New York (C. J.)	F. Roosevelt	06/12/1941	06/21/1941	06/23/1941	Reported favorably	06/27/1941	Confirmed	9	11	15
James F. Byrnes of South Carolina	F. Roosevelt	06/12/1941	Nomination was not referred to Judiciary Committee.			06/12/1941	Confirmed	—	—	0
Robert H. Jackson of New York	F. Roosevelt	06/12/1941	06/21/1941	06/30/1941	Reported favorably	07/07/1941	Confirmed	9	18	25
Wiley B. Rutledge of Iowa	F. Roosevelt	01/11/1943	01/22/1943	02/01/1943	Reported favorably	02/08/1943	Confirmed	11	21	28

Table 1. Nominations to the Supreme Court of the United States, 1789-2005 (Continued)

Nominee	President	Date received in Senate [a]	Senate committee actions			Final action by Senate or President		Days from date received in Senate to:		
			Public hearing date(s)	Final vote date [b]	Final vote	Date	Final action [c]	First hearing date	Committee final vote date	Final action by Senate or President
Harold H. Burton of Ohio	Truman	09/18/1945	No record of hearing	09/19/1945	Reported favorably	09/19/1945	Confirmed	—	1	1
Fred M. Vinson of Kentucky (C. J.)	Truman	06/06/1946	06/14/1946	06/19/1946	Reported favorably	06/20/1946	Confirmed	8	13	14
Tom C. Clark of Texas	Truman	08/02/1949	08/09/1949 08/10/1949 08/11/1949	08/12/1949	Reported favorably (9-2)	08/18/1949	Confirmed (73-8)	7	10	16
Sherman Minton of Indiana	Truman	09/15/1949	09/27/1949	10/03/1949	Reported favorably (9-2)	Motion to recommit rejected, 10/04/1949 (21-45)		12	18	19
						10/04/1949	Confirmed (48-16)			
Earl Warren of California (C. J.)	Eisenhower	*Recess Appointment, 10/02/1953*								
		01/11/1954	02/02/1954 02/19/1954	02/24/1954	Reported favorably (12-3)	03/01/1954	Confirmed	22	44	49
John M. Harlan II of New York	Eisenhower	11/09/1954	No record of hearing	Referred to Judiciary Committee on 11/09/1954. No record of committee vote or Senate action.					—	—
John M. Harlan II of New York	Eisenhower	01/10/1955	02/25/1955[g]	03/10/1955	Reported favorably (10-4)	03/16/1955	Confirmed (71-11)	45	59	65
William J. Brennan Jr. of New Jersey	Eisenhower	*Recess Appointment, 10/15/1956*								
		01/14/1957	02/26/1957 02/27/1957	03/04/1957	Reported favorably	03/19/1957	Confirmed	43	49	64

Table 1. Nominations to the Supreme Court of the United States, 1789-2005 (Continued)

Nominee	President	Date received in Senate [a]	Senate committee actions			Final action by Senate or President		Days from date received in Senate to:		
			Public hearing date(s)	Final vote date [b]	Final vote	Date	Final action [c]	First hearing date	Committee final vote date	Final action by Senate or President
Charles E. Whittaker of Missouri	Eisenhower	03/02/1957	03/18/1957	03/18/1957	Reported favorably	03/19/1957	Confirmed	16	16	17
Potter Stewart of Ohio	Eisenhower	*Recess Appointment, 10/14/1958*								
		01/17/1959	04/09/1959 04/14/1959	04/20/1959	Reported favorably (12-3)	05/05/1959	Confirmed (70-17)	82	93	108
Byron R. White of Colorado	Kennedy	04/03/1962	04/11/1962	04/11/1962	Reported favorably	04/11/1962	Confirmed	8	8	8
Arthur J. Goldberg of Illinois	Kennedy	08/31/1962	09/11/1962 09/13/1962	09/25/1962	Reported favorably	09/25/1962	Confirmed	11	25	25
Abe Fortas of Tennessee	L. Johnson	07/28/1965	08/05/1965	08/10/1965	Reported favorably	08/11/1965	Confirmed	8	13	14
Thurgood Marshall of New York	L. Johnson	06/13/1967	07/13/1967 07/14/1967 07/18/1967 07/19/1967 07/24/1967	08/03/1967	Reported favorably (11-5)	08/30/1967	Confirmed (69-11)	30	51	78
Abe Fortas of Tennessee (C. J.)	L. Johnson	06/26/1968	07/11/1968 07/12/1968 07/16/1968 07/17/1968 07/18/1968 07/19/1968 07/20/1968 07/22/1968 07/23/1968 09/13/1968 09/16/1968	09/17/1968	Reported favorably (11-6)	Cloture motion rejected, 10/01/1968 (45-43) [h]		15	83	100
						10/04/1968	Withdrawn			

Table 1. Nominations to the Supreme Court of the United States, 1789-2005 (Continued)

Nominee	President	Date received in Senate [a]	Senate committee actions			Final action by Senate or President		Days from date received in Senate to:		
			Public hearing date(s)	Final vote date [b]	Final vote	Date	Final action [c]	First hearing date	Committee final vote date	Final action by Senate or President
Homer Thornberry of Texas	L. Johnson	06/26/1968	07/11/1968 07/12/1968 07/16/1968 07/17/1968 07/18/1968 07/19/1968 07/20/1968 07/22/1968 07/23/1968 09/13/1968 09/16/1968	Referred to Judiciary Committee on 06/26/1968. No committee vote taken.		10/04/1968	Withdrawn	15	—	100
Warren E. Burger of Virginia (C. J.)	Nixon	05/23/1969	06/03/1969	06/03/1969	Reported favorably	06/09/1969	Confirmed (74-3)	11	11	17
Clement F. Haynsworth Jr. of South Carolina	Nixon	09/03/1969	09/16/1969 09/17/1969 09/18/1969 09/19/1969 09/23/1969 09/24/1969 09/25/1969 0926/1969	10/09/1969	Reported favorably (10-7)	11/21/1969	Rejected (45-55)	13	36	79
George Harrold Carswell of Florida	Nixon	01/19/1970	01/27/1970 01/28/1970 01/29/1970 02/02/1970 02/03/1970	02/16/1970	Reported favorably (13-4)	04/08/1970	Rejected (45-51)	8	28	79
Harry A. Blackmun of Minnesota	Nixon	04/15/1970	04/29/1970	05/06/1970	Reported favorably (17-0)	05/12/1970	Confirmed (94-0)	14	21	27

Table 1. Nominations to the Supreme Court of the United States, 1789-2005 (Continued)

Nominee	President	Date received in Senate [a]	Senate committee actions			Final action by Senate or President		Days from date received in Senate to:		
			Public hearing date(s)	Final vote date [b]	Final vote	Date	Final action [c]	First hearing date	Committee final vote date	Final action by Senate or President
Lewis F. Powell Jr. of Virginia	Nixon	10/22/1971	11/03/1971 11/04/1971 11/08/1971 11/09/1971 11/10/1971	11/23/1971	Reported favorably (16-0)	12/06/1971	Confirmed (89-1)	12	32	45
William H. Rehnquist of Arizona	Nixon	10/22/1971	11/03/1971 11/04/1971 11/08/1971 11/09/1971 11/10/1971	11/23/1971	Reported favorably (12-4)	Cloture motion rejected, 12/10/1971 (52-42) [i] Motion to postpone until 01/18/1972 rejected, 12/10/1971 (22-70)		12	32	49
						12/10/1971	Confirmed (68-26)			
John Paul Stevens of Illinois	Ford	12/01/1975 (Nom. date 11/28/1975)	12/08/1975 12/09/1975 12/10/1975	12/11/1975	Reported favorably (13-0)	12/17/1975	Confirmed (98-0)	7	10	16
Sandra Day O'Connor of Arizona	Reagan	08/19/1981	09/09/1981 09/10/1981 09/11/1981	09/15/1981	Reported favorably (17-1)	09/21/1981	Confirmed (99-0)	21	27	33
William H. Rehnquist of Arizona (C. J.)	Reagan	06/20/1986	07/29/1986 07/30/1986 07/31/1986 08/01/1986	08/14/1986	Reported favorably (13-5)	Cloture invoked, 09/17/1986 (68-31) [j]		39	55	89
						09/17/1986	Confirmed (65-33)			
Antonin Scalia of Virginia	Reagan	06/24/1986	08/05/1986 08/06/1986	08/14/1986	Reported favorably (18-0)	09/17/1986	Confirmed (98-0)	42	51	85

Table 1. Nominations to the Supreme Court of the United States, 1789-2005 (Continued)

<table>
<tr><th rowspan="2">Nominee</th><th rowspan="2">President</th><th rowspan="2">Date received in Senate [a]</th><th colspan="3">Senate committee actions</th><th colspan="2">Final action by Senate or President</th><th colspan="3">Days from date received in Senate to:</th></tr>
<tr><th>Public hearing date(s)</th><th>Final vote date [b]</th><th>Final vote</th><th>Date</th><th>Final action [c]</th><th>First hearing date</th><th>Committee final vote date</th><th>Final action by Senate or President</th></tr>
<tr><td rowspan="2">Robert H. Bork
of District of Columbia</td><td rowspan="2">Reagan</td><td rowspan="2">07/07/1987</td><td rowspan="2">09/15/1987
09/16/1987
09/17/1987
09/18/1987
09/19/1987
09/21/1987
09/22/1987
09/23/1987
09/25/1987
09/28/1987
09/29/1987
09/30/1987</td><td colspan="2">Motion to report favorably rejected, 10/06/1987 (5-9)</td><td rowspan="2">10/23/1987</td><td rowspan="2">Rejected (42-58)</td><td rowspan="2">70</td><td rowspan="2">91</td><td rowspan="2">108</td></tr>
<tr><td>10/06/1987</td><td>Reported unfavorably (9-5)</td></tr>
<tr><td>Anthony M. Kennedy
of California</td><td>Reagan</td><td>11/30/1987</td><td>12/14/1987
12/15/1987
12/16/1987</td><td>01/27/1988</td><td>Reported favorably (14-0)</td><td>02/03/1988</td><td>Confirmed (97-0)</td><td>14</td><td>58</td><td>65</td></tr>
<tr><td>David H. Souter
of New Hampshire</td><td>G. H. W. Bush</td><td>07/25/1990</td><td>09/13/1990
09/14/1990
09/17/1990
09/18/1990
09/19/1990</td><td>09/27/1990</td><td>Reported favorably (13-1)</td><td>10/02/1990</td><td>Confirmed (90-9)</td><td>50</td><td>64</td><td>69</td></tr>
<tr><td rowspan="2">Clarence Thomas
of Virginia</td><td rowspan="2">G. H. W. Bush</td><td rowspan="2">07/08/1991</td><td rowspan="2">09/10/1991
09/11/1991
09/12/1991
09/13/1991
09/16/1991
09/17/1991
09/19/1991
09/20/1991
10/11/1991
10/12/1991
10/13/1991</td><td colspan="2">Motion to report favorably failed, 09/27/1991 (7-7) [k]</td><td colspan="2">UC agreement reached, 10/08/1991, to reschedule vote on confirmation from 10/08/1991 to 10/15/991, to allow for additional hearings</td><td rowspan="2">64</td><td rowspan="2">81</td><td rowspan="2">99</td></tr>
<tr><td>09/27/1991</td><td>Reported without recommen-dation (13-1)</td><td>10/15/1991</td><td>Confirmed (52-48)</td></tr>
</table>

Table 1. Nominations to the Supreme Court of the United States, 1789-2005 (Continued)

Nominee	President	Date received in Senate [a]	Senate committee actions			Final action by Senate or President		Days from date received in Senate to:		
			Public hearing date(s)	Final vote date [b]	Final vote	Date	Final action [c]	First hearing date	Committee final vote date	Final action by Senate or President
Ruth Bader Ginsburg of New York	Clinton	06/22/1993	07/20/1993 07/21/1993 07/22/1993 07/23/1993	07/29/1993	Reported favorably (18-0)	08/03/1993	Confirmed (96-3)	28	37	42
Stephen G. Breyer of Massachusetts	Clinton	05/17/1994	07/12/1994 07/13/1994 07/14/1994 07/15/1994	07/19/1994	Reported favorably (18-0)	07/29/1994	Confirmed (87-9)	56	63	73
John G. Roberts Jr. of Maryland	G. W. Bush	07/29/2005	Referred to Judiciary Committee on 07/29/2005. No hearing held and no committee vote taken.			09/06/2005	Withdrawn	—	—	39
John G. Roberts Jr. of Maryland (C. J.)	G. W. Bush	09/06/2005	09/12/2005 09/13/2005 09/14/2005 09/15/2005	09/22/2005	Reported favorably (13-5)	09/29/2005	Confirmed (78-22)	6	16	23
Harriet E. Miers of Texas	G. W. Bush	10/07/2005	Referred to Judiciary Committee on 10/07/2005. No hearing held and no committee vote taken.			10/28/2005	Withdrawn	—	—	21
Samuel A. Alito Jr.	G. W. Bush	11/10/2005	Referred to Judiciary Committee on 11/10/2005. Hearings scheduled to begin on 01/09/2006.							
Median number of days from date received in Senate, 1789-2005								13	11	10
Median number of days from date received in Senate, 1789-1966								11	9	7
Median number of days from date received in Senate, 1967-2005								15	37	67

Sources: U.S. Congress, Senate, Journal of the Executive Proceedings of the Senate of the United States of America (hereafter, Senate Executive Journal), various editions from the 1st Congress through the 107th Congress; Senate Committee on the Judiciary, Legislative and Executive Calendar, various editions from the 77th Congress through the 103rd Congress; various newspaper accounts accessed on-line through ProQuest Historical Newspapers (the primary source for recorded vote tallies in committee prior to the 1980s); and CRS Report RL31171, Supreme Court Nominations Not Confirmed, 1789-2005, by Henry B. Hogue.

a. Usually the date on which the President formally makes a nomination, by signing a nomination message, is the same as the date on which the nomination is received, and these two dates are the same for any given nomination when only one date is shown in the "Date received in Senate" column. However, for the occasional nomination made by a President on a date prior to the nomination's receipt by the Senate, the earlier presidential nomination date ("Nom. date") is distinguished, in parentheses, from the date when the nomination was received by the Senate.

b. For nominations prior to 1873 that were referred to committee, the "Final vote date" is the date recorded in the Senate Executive Journal on which the committee's chairman or other member reported the nomination to the Senate. For nominations from 1873 to 2005, the "Final vote date" is the date on which the Judiciary Committee voted to report a nomination or, in one instance (on Feb. 14 1881) involving the first Stanley Matthews nomination), voted to postpone taking taking action.

c. "Final action," for purposes of this table, covers the following mutually exclusive outcomes: confirmation by the Senate ("Confirmed"), withdrawal of a nomination by the President ("Withdrawn") and Senate rejection by a vote disapproving a nomination ("Rejected"). In other instances, when none of the preceding three outcomes occurred, the last procedural action taken by the Senate on a nomination is indicated. On certain nominations, as indicated in the table, the last procedural outcome entailed tabling a nomination ("Tabled"), postponing consideration ("Postponed"), or rejecting a motion to proceed to consideration ("Motion to proceed rejected"). Final Senate actions taken by roll-call votes are shown in parentheses. Final Senate actions without roll-call votes shown in parentheses were reached by voice vote or unanimous consent. For roll-call votes shown above, the number of Yea votes always comes before the number of Nay votes. Thus, under "Confirmed" or "Rejected," the first number in the vote tally is the number of Senators who voted in favor of confirmation, and the second the number voting against confirmation.

d. On Dec. 16 and 17, 1873, the Judiciary Committee held closed-door sessions to examine documents and hear testimony from witnesses relevant to a controversy that arose over the Williams nomination only after the committee had reported the nomination to the Senate. The controversy prompted the Senate to recommit the nomination to the Judiciary Committee and to authorize the committee "to send for persons and papers." Senate Executive Journal, vol. 19, p. 211. After holding the two closed- door sessions , the committee did not re-report the nomination to the Senate. Amid press reports of significant opposition to the nomination in both the Judiciary Committee and the Senate as a whole, the nomination, at Williams's request, was withdrawn by President Ulysses S. Grant on Jan. 8, 1874. The Dec. 16 and 17 sessions can be regarded as an early, perhaps the earliest, example of a Judiciary Committee closed-door hearing. However, the above table, which focuses in part on the times that elapsed between dates nominations were received in the Senate and dates of public confirmation hearings, does not count the time that elapsed from the date the Williams nominations was received in the Senate until the Dec. 16 and 17, 1873, sessions, because they were closed to the public.

e. The 60-4 roll call vote to confirm Taft, conducted by the Senate in closed-door executive session, was not recorded in the Senate Executive Journal. Newspaper accounts, however, reported that a roll call vote on the nomination was demanded in the executive session, and that the vote was 60-4 to confirm, with an agreement reached afterwards not to make the roll call public. See Robert J. Bender, "Ex-President Taft New Chief Justice of United States," Atlanta Constitution, July 1, 1921, p. 1; Charles S. Groves, "Taft Is Confirmed, as Chief Justice," Boston Daily Globe, July 1, 1921, p. 1; and "Proceedings of Congress and Committees in Brief," Washington Post, July 1, 1921, p. 6.

f. The Jan. 12, 1925, hearing, held in closed session, heard the testimony of former Sen. Willard Saulsbury of Delaware. "Nomination of Stone Is Held Up Once More," New York Times, Jan. 13, 1925, p. 4. At the Jan. 28, 1925, hearing, which was held in open session, the nominee was questioned by the Judiciary Committee for four hours. This was the first confirmation hearing for a Supreme Court nomination at which the nominee appeared in person to testify. See Albert W. Fox, "Stone Tells Senate Committee He Assumes Full Responsibility for Pressing New Wheeler Case," Washington Post, Jan. 29, 1925, p. 1.

g. The Judiciary Committee held two days of confirmation hearings on the Harlan nomination, on Feb. 24 and 25, 1955. The Feb. 24 session, held in closed session, heard the testimony of nine witnesses (seven in favor of confirmation, and two opposed). Luther A. Huston, "Harlan Hearing Held by Senators," New York Times, Feb. 25, 1955, p. 8. The committee also began the Feb. 25 hearing in closed session, to hear the testimony of additional witnesses. However, for Judge Harlan, who was the last scheduled witness, the committee "voted to open the hearing to newspaper reporters for his testimony." Luther A. Huston, "Harlan Disavows 'One World' Aims in Senate Inquiry," New York Times, Feb. 26, 1955, p. 1.

h. The 45 votes in favor of the motion to close debate fell far short of the super-majority required under Senate rules — then two-thirds of Senators present and voting. The cloture motion, if approved, would have closed a lengthy debate (which had consumed more than 25 hours over a four-day period) on a motion to proceed to consider the Fortas nomination.

i. The 52 votes in favor of the motion to close debate fell short of the super-majority required under Senate rules — then two-thirds of Senators present and voting. Although the cloture motion failed, the Senate later that day (Dec. 10, 1971) agreed, without a procedural vote, to close debate and then voted to confirm Rehnquist 68-26.

j. The 68 votes in favor of the motion to close debate, by invoking cloture, exceeded the majority required under Senate rules — then, and currently, three-fifths of the Senate's full membership.

k. Motions to gain approval in Senate committees require a majority vote in favor and thus fail if there is a tie vote.

Table 2. Senate Votes on Whether to Confirm Supreme Court Nominations: Number Made by Voice Vote/Unanimous Consent (UC) or by Roll-Call Vote

Years	By voice vote or UC (all to confirm)	By roll-call vote (votes to reject in parentheses)	Totals
1789-1829	24	4 (2)	28
1830-1889	15	21 (3)	36
1890-1965	34	16 (3)	50
1966-2005	0	18 (3)	18
Totals	73	59 (11)	132 (11)

Sources: U.S. Congress, Senate, *Journal of the Executive Proceedings of the Senate of the United States of America,* various editions from the 1st Congress through the 107th Congress; also, "Nominations" database in the Legislative Information System, available at [http://www.congress.gov/nomis/].

References

[1] On Nov. 10, 2005, President George W. Bush nominated a U.S. appellate court judge, Samuel A. Alito Jr., to be an Associate Justice of the Supreme Court. The Senate Judiciary Committee has scheduled confirmation hearings on the nomination to begin on Jan. 9, 2006.

[2] Specifically, eight persons were nominated twice to the same Court position (seven to be Associate Justice, one to be Chief Justice); one person was nominated three times to be Associate Justice; and nine persons were nominated first to be Associate Justice and later to be Chief Justice. The sum of 19 (the number of Court nominations that were not a person's first nomination to the Court) and 139 (the number of persons nominated to the Court at least once) is 158 (total Supreme Court nominations).

[3] The nation's first Chief Justice, John Jay, was nominated to that position twice. Jay was first nominated, and confirmed, in September 1789. He resigned as Chief Justice in 1795 to serve as governor of New York. In December 1800, Jay was nominated and confirmed a second time as Chief Justice, but declined the appointment. For analysis of the process by which a Chief Justice is appointed, accompanied by a list of all Chief Justice nominations from 1789 to the present (including the nomination, confirmation, judicial oath, and end-of-service dates of Chief Justice nominees, as well as their ages at time of appointment and upon termination of service), see CRS Report RL32821, *The Chief Justice of the United*

States: Responsibilities of the Office and Process for Appointment, by Denis Steven Rutkus and Lorraine H. Tong.

[4] The three Presidents not to have made any Supreme Court nominations were William Henry Harrison, Zachary Taylor, and Jimmy Carter, with no Court vacancies having occurred while they were in office. See "Table 3. Supreme Court Nominations, by President, 1789 to October 2005," in CRS Report RL31171, *Supreme Court Nominations Not Confirmed, 1789-2005,* by Henry B. Hogue, which lists the number of vacancies on the Court that existed during each presidency, from George Washington to George W. Bush. While it is unremarkable that no vacancies occurred during the short-lived presidencies of Harrison (Mar. 4 to Apr. 4, 1841) and Taylor (Mar. 5, 1849 to July 9, 1850), Jimmy Carter's presidency (Jan. 20, 1977, to Jan. 20, 1981) is remarkable as the only one lasting a full term during which no Supreme Court vacancies occurred.

[5] See Myron Jacobstein and Roy M. Mersky, *The Rejected* (Milpitas, CA: Toucan Valley Publications, 1993), pp. 69-74. (Hereafter cited as Jacobstein and Mersky, *The Rejected.*)

[6] The five Presidents whose single Supreme Court nominations received Senate confirmation were Franklin Pierce, James A. Garfield, William McKinley, Calvin Coolidge, and Gerald R. Ford. As mentioned above, the one President whose single Court nomination did not receive confirmation was Andrew Johnson.

[7] A President may announce the selection of a nominee well before transmitting a nomination message to the Senate. For instance, President George W. Bush announced his selection of Samuel A. Alito Jr. to be a Supreme Court nominee on Oct. 31, 2005, but formally signed and transmitted the nomination of Alito to the Senate on Nov. 10, 2005. For a complete list, from 1900 to 2005, of the dates on which Presidents announced their Supreme Court nominees (as distinguished from when they signed and transmitted nomination documents to the Senate), see CRS Report RL33118, *Speed of Presidential and Senate Actions on Supreme Court Nominations, 1900-2005*, by R. Sam Garrett, Denis Steven Rutkus, and Curtis W. Copeland.

[8] See U.S. Congress, Senate Committee on the Judiciary, *History of the Committee on the Judiciary, United States Senate, 1816-1981.* Sen. Doc. No. 97-18, 97th Cong., 1st sess. (Washington: GPO, 1982), p. iv; also, U.S. Senate, *History of the Committee on Rules and Administration — United States Senate,* prepared by Floyd M. Riddick, Parliamentarian Emeritus of the Senate, 96th Cong., 1st sess., S. Doc. No. 96-27 (Washington: GPO,

1980). Riddick provides, on pp. 21-28, the full text of the general revision of the Senate rules, adopted in 1868, including, on p. 26, the following rule: "When nominations shall be made by the President of the United States to the Senate, they shall, unless otherwise ordered by the Senate, be referred to appropriate committees .... "

[9] The nominations from 1868 to the present not referred to the Judiciary Committee were those of: Edwin M. Stanton in 1869 (at time of nomination, former Secretary of War); Edward D. White in 1894 (Senator); Joseph M. McKenna in 1897 (Attorney General, and former U.S. Representative); Edward D. White again, in 1910, this time to be Chief Justice (Associate Justice at time of nomination, and former Senator); William Howard Taft in 1921 (former President); George Sutherland in 1922 (former Senator); and James F. Byrnes in 1941 (Senator).

[10] At least once in the 19th century, however, in 1873, the Judiciary Committee did hear witnesses testify concerning a Supreme Court nomination — that of George H. Williams to be Chief Justice — but these two days of hearings, on Dec. 16 and 17, 1873, were held in closed session. The closed-door sessions were held to examine documents and hear testimony from witnesses relevant to a controversy that arose over the Williams nomination only after the committee had reported the nomination to the Senate. The controversy prompted the Senate to recommit the nomination to the Judiciary Committee and to authorize the committee "to send for persons and papers." U.S. Congress, Senate, *Journal of the Executive Proceedings of the Senate of the United States of America*, vol. 19 (Washington: GPO, 1901), p. 189. After holding the two closed-door sessions on Dec. 16 and 17, the committee did not re-report the nomination to the Senate. Amid press reports of significant opposition to the nomination both in the Judiciary Committee and the Senate as a whole, the nomination, at Williams's request, was withdrawn by President Ulysses S. Grant on Jan. 8, 1874. See Jacobstein and Mersky, *The Rejected*, pp. 82-87.

[11] For a discussion of the advent of Supreme Court nominee appearances before the Senate Judiciary Committee, starting with Harlan F. Stone in 1925 (and carrying through the nominations of Abe Fortas and Homer Thornberry in 1968), see James A.Thorpe, *of Public Law,* vol. 18, 1969, pp. 371-402.

[12] A scholar examining the procedures followed by the committee in its consideration of 15 Supreme Court nominations referred to it between 1923 and 1947 found that, with two exceptions — the nominations of Charles Evans Hughes in 1930 and Harold H. Burton to be Associate Justices in

1945 — all of the nominations were first "processed by a subcommittee prior to consideration by the full committee membership." David Gregg Farrelly, "Operational Aspects of the Senate Judiciary Committee," (Ph.D. diss., Princeton University: 1949), pp. 184-185. (Hereafter cited as Farrelly, "Operational Aspects.")

[13] The five other nominations not receiving confirmation hearings even though referred to the Judiciary Committee were of former New York governor and former Supreme Court Associate Justice Charles Evans Hughes in 1930; former federal prosecutor Owen J. Roberts in 1930; Senator Hugo L. Black in 1937; Attorney General and former Michigan governor Frank Murphy in 1940; and former Senator Harold H. Burton in 1945.

[14] For example, a Judiciary subcommittee hearing on the 1932 nomination of Benjamin N. Cardozo lasted only five minutes, during which one witness testified in opposition. Likewise, when the Judiciary Committee extended open invitations for witnesses to testify in opposition at the confirmation hearings for Stanley F. Reed in 1938, William O. Douglas in 1939, Harlan F. Stone (for Chief Justice) in 1941, and Wiley B. Rutledge in 1943, no witnesses appeared to protest against Douglas or Stone, and "only one or two persons filed protests" against Reed and Rutledge. Farrelly, "Operational Aspects," pp. 194-195.

[15] The last Supreme Court nomination on which a Senate Judiciary subcommittee held hearings was the 1954 nomination of Earl Warren to be Chief Justice. The subcommittee held public hearings on the nomination on Feb. 2 and 19, 1954, after which the full committee, on Feb. 24, 1954, voted to report the nomination favorably. All subsequent hearings on Supreme Court nominations were held by the full Judiciary Committee.

[16] The Judiciary Committee held two days of confirmation hearings on the second Harlan nomination, on Feb. 24 and 25, 1955. The Feb. 24 session, held in *closed* session, heard the testimony of nine witnesses (seven in favor of confirmation, and two opposed). Luther A. Huston, "Harlan Hearing Held by Senators," *New York Times,* Feb. 25, 1955, p. 8. The committee also began the Feb. 25 hearing in closed session, to hear the testimony of additional witnesses. However, for Judge Harlan, who was the last scheduled witness, the committee "voted to open the hearing to newspaper reporters for his testimony." Luther A. Huston, "Harlan Disavows 'One World' Aims in Senate Inquiry," *New York Times,* Feb. 26, 1955, p. 1.

[17] These were the nominations of Robert H. Bork in 1987 (12 hearing days), Clarence Thomas in 1991 (11 days), and Abe Fortas and Homer Thornberry in 1968 (11 days for their joint hearings).

[18] In 1969, eight days of confirmation hearings were held on the nomination of Clement F. Haynsworth.

[19] One day of hearings each was held on the nominations of Warren E. Burger (to be Chief Justice) in 1969 and Harry A. Blackmun in 1970, while two days of hearings were held on the nomination of Antonin Scalia in 1986.

[20] As noted earlier, only once prior to the establishment of the Judiciary Committee in 1816 was a Supreme Court nomination referred to committee, and that nomination was reported to the Senate as well. See in Table 1 the nomination in 1811 of Alexander Wolcott, which was considered by a select committee and then reported to the Senate, where it was rejected by a 9-24 vote.

[21] The six favorably reported nominations which failed to receive Senate confirmation involved these nominees: George H. Williams, for Chief Justice, in 1873 (nomination withdrawn); Caleb Cushing, in 1874 (nomination withdrawn); Pierce Butler in 1922 (no action taken by Senate); Abe Fortas, for Chief Justice, in 1968 (nomination withdrawn); Clement F. Haynsworth Jr. in 1969 (rejected by Senate); and G. Harrold Carswell in 1970 (rejected by Senate). Butler, it should be noted, was re-nominated and confirmed.

[22] A report that states it is not accompanied by a recommendation can be a way to alert the Senate that a substantial number of committee members have some reservations about the nominee which, however, do not rise, at that point, to the level of opposition; it might also be a way, for reporting purposes, to bridge or downplay differences between committee members who favor confirmation and other members who oppose it.

[23] The three nominees confirmed by the Senate after the Judiciary Committee explicitly reported their nominations without recommendation were: Melville W. Fuller, for Chief Justice, in 1888; George Shiras Jr. in 1892; and Clarence Thomas in 1991. A fourth nomination reported without recommendation, Wheeler H. Peckham, in 1894, was rejected by the Senate.

[24] See in Table 1 the second nomination of Stanley Matthews in 1881 (confirmed 24-23) and the nomination of Lucius Q. C. Lamar in 1888 (confirmed 32-28).

[25] The nominations reported unfavorably and then rejected by the Senate involved these nominees: Ebenezer R. Hoar in 1869 (rejected 24-33); William B. Hornblower in 1894 (rejected 24-30); John J. Parker in 1930 (rejected 39-41); and Robert H. Bork in 1987 (rejected 42-58).

[26] The Senate in 1829 postponed taking action on the nomination of John Crittenden after receiving an adverse report on the nomination from the Judiciary Committee.

[27] In 1853, the nomination of William C. Micou was referred to the Judiciary Committee and on the same day ordered discharged by the Senate, where no action was taken. In 1866, the nomination of Henry Stanbery was referred to the Judiciary Committee, but shortly afterwards, while the nomination was pending in the Senate, the Associate Justice position to which Stanbery had been nominated was eliminated by statute. In 1893, the nomination of William B. Hornblower was referred to the Judiciary Committee, but not reported; later that year, in a new session of Congress, Hornblower was re-nominated, reported unfavorably by the Judiciary Committee (in early 1894), and rejected by the Senate, 24-30. In 1968, the Judiciary Committee declined to report the nomination of Homer Thornberry to succeed Associate Justice Abe Fortas until the final outcome of the nomination of Fortas to be Chief Justice was determined. The Thornberry and Fortas nominations were both withdrawn by the President after a motion to close debate on the Fortas nomination failed to pass in the Senate. (The failure of Fortas's Chief Justice nomination eliminated the prospective Associate Justice vacancy that Thornberry had been nominated to fill.) In 2005, the nomination of Harriet E. Miers was withdrawn by the President before the Judiciary Committee held hearings on the nomination.

[28] In February 1881, just before the final adjournment of the 46th Congress, the Judiciary Committee voted to postpone taking action on the Supreme Court nomination of Stanley Matthews; shortly afterwards, however, in a special session of the 47th Congress, Matthews was re-nominated, and, although his second nomination was reported unfavorably by the Judiciary Committee, it was confirmed by the Senate, 24-23. In Nov. 1954, late in the 83rd Congress, the nomination of John M. Harlan II was referred to the Judiciary Committee, where no action was taken; in 1955, Harlan was re-nominated, considered and reported favorably by the Judiciary Committee, and confirmed by the Senate. In Sept. 2005, before the scheduled start of confirmation hearings, the nomination of John G. Roberts Jr. to be Associate Justice was withdrawn and, on the same day of the withdrawal, Roberts was renominated for Chief Justice; the second Roberts nomination was reported favorably by the Judiciary Committee and confirmed by the Senate.

[29] The exact confirmation percentage is 77.1%, reached by dividing 121 confirmations by 157 nominations (excluding the 158th nomination of Samuel A. Alito Jr.).

[30] The earliest Senate rejection of a Supreme Court nomination occurred in 1795, when President George Washington's nomination of John Rutledge to be Chief Justice failed on a 10-14 vote. The latest instance was the Senate's rejection of Robert H. Bork in 1987, by a 42-58 vote. Between Rutledge and Bork, the following nominations were also rejected: Alexander Wolcott in 1811, John C. Spencer in 1844, George W. Woodward in 1846, Ebenezer R. Hoar in 1870, William B. Hornblower in 1894, Wheeler H. Peckham in 1894, John J. Parker in 1930, Clement F. Haynsworth Jr. in 1969, and G. Harrold Carswell in 1970.

[31] The following Supreme Court nominations were withdrawn, in the years indicated, with the Presidents who withdrew them shown in parentheses: The first nomination of William Paterson, in 1793 (George Washington); the first nomination of Reuben H. Walworth, in 1844 (John Tyler); the second nomination of John C. Spencer, in 1844 (John Tyler); the third nomination of Reuben H. Walworth, in 1845 (John Tyler); the second nomination of Edward King, in 1845 (John Tyler); George H. Williams and Caleb Cushing, both in 1874 (Ulysses S. Grant); Abe Fortas and Homer Thornberry, both in 1968 (Lyndon B. Johnson); John G. Roberts Jr. and Harrier E. Miers, both in 2005 (George W. Bush). Less than a week after his first nomination was withdrawn, Paterson was re-nominated by President Washington and confirmed by the Senate on the same day. On the same day that President Bush withdrew the Roberts nomination to be Associate Justice, he re-nominated Roberts to be Chief Justice, and the latter nomination was confirmed.

[32] The 14 nominations that lapsed at the end of a session of Congress, without a Senate confirmation or rejection vote or a withdrawal by the President having occurred, can be broken into the following groups according to Senate actions, or lack of Senate actions, taken: On three nominations (John Crittenden in 1829, the first nomination of Roger Taney in 1835, and George E. Badger in 1853), the Senate voted to postpone taking action; the Senate tabled two nominations (the first nomination of Edward King in 1844 and Edward A. Bradford in 1852); on one nomination, the Senate rejected a motion to proceed (Jeremiah S. Black in 1861, by a 25-26 vote); and on eight nominations, there was no record of any vote taken (the second nomination of Reuben H. Walworth in 1844, John M. Read in 1845, William C. Micou in 1853, Henry Stanbery in 1866, the first nomination of

Stanley Matthews in 1881, the first nomination of William B. Hornblower in 1893, the first nomination of Pierce Butler in 1922, and the first nomination of John M. Harlan II in 1954). However, four of the 14 persons whose nominations lapsed in one session of Congress were re-nominated in the next congressional session and confirmed (Taney in 1835, Matthews in 1881, Butler in 1922, and Harlan in 1955).

[33] The closest roll calls ever cast on Supreme Court nominations were the 24-23 vote in 1881 confirming Stanley Matthews, the 25-26 vote in 1861 rejecting a motion to proceed to consider the nomination of Jeremiah S. Black, and the 26-25 Senate vote in 1853 to postpone consideration of the nomination of George E. Badger. Since the 1960s, the closest roll calls on Supreme Court nominations were the 52-48 vote in 1991 confirming Clarence Thomas, the 45-51 vote in 1970 rejecting G. Harrold Carswell, the 45-55 vote in 1969 rejecting Clement Haynsworth Jr., the 42-58 vote in 1987 rejecting Robert H. Bork, and the 65-33 vote confirming William H. Rchnquist to bc Chicf Justicc in 1986. Also noteworthy was the 45-43 vote in 1968 rejecting a motion to close debate on the nomination of Abe Fortas to be Chief Justice; however, the roll call was not as close as the numbers by themselves suggested, since passage of the motion required a two-thirds vote of the Members present and voting.

[34] The most lopsided of these votes were the unanimous roll calls confirming Morrison R. Waite to be Chief Justice in 1874 (63-0), Harry A. Blackmun in 1970 (94-0), John Paul Stevens in 1975 (98-0), Sandra Day O'Connor in 1981 (99-0), Antonin Scalia in 1986 (98-0), and Anthony M. Kennedy in 1988 (97-0); and the near-unanimous votes confirming Noah H. Swayne in 1862 (38-1),Warren E. Burger in 1969 to be Chief Justice (74-3), Lewis F. Powell Jr. in 1971 (89-1), and Ruth Bader Ginsburg in 1993 (96-3).

[35] In calculating the median elapsed time for the contemporary period, the Marshall nomination in 1967 was selected as the starting point for the following reason. The Marshall nomination, it could be argued, marked the start of an era in which the confirmation hearings of most, if not all, Supreme Court nominees were highly charged events, covered closely by the news media, with nominees interrogated rigorously and extensively (and for more than a day) about their judicial philosophy as well as their views on constitutional issues and the proper role of the Supreme Court in the U.S. government. For the Marshall nomination, the elapsed time between Senate receipt and start of confirmation hearings was 30 days.

[36] See bottom rows of Table 1 for median number of days that elapsed from the date Supreme Court nominations were received in the Senate to first hearing dates, for three different time spans.

[37] For the four nominations, the elapsed time between Senate receipt of nomination and the first day of confirmation hearings was 50 days for David Souter in 1990, 64 days for Clarence Thomas in 1991, 28 days for Ruth Bader Ginsburg in 1993, and 56 days for Stephen G. Breyer in 1994.

[38] As already mentioned, the first such nomination, of Alexander Wolcott in 1811, was reported by a select committee; all subsequently reported nominations were reported by the Senate Judiciary Committee.

[39] Ironically, five days after the committee's favorable, and extremely prompt, recommendation of Cushing, President Ulysses S. Grant withdrew the nomination.

[40] Five nominations were voted on by the Judiciary Committee one day after their receipt by the Senate: Robert C. Grier in 1846; John A. Campbell in 1853; Morrison R. Waite, to be Chief Justice, in 1874; Horace Gray in 1881; and Harold H. Burton in 1945. Six nominations were voted on by the committee two days after Senate receipt: James M. Wayne in 1835; Samuel Nelson in 1845; Noah H. Swayne in 1862; David Davis in 1862; Stephen J. Field in 1963; and Oliver Wendell Holmes in 1902. Three nominations were voted on by the committee three days after Senate receipt: Horace H. Lurton in 1909; Willis Van Devanter in 1910; and Joseph R. Lamar in 1910.

[41] The first of Reuben H. Walworth's three nominations to the Court in 1844 was voted on by the Judiciary Committee 93 days after Senate receipt and committee referral. During the 20th century, the Judiciary Committee, in addition to its 1916 vote on the Brandeis nomination, voted on the following nominations more than 80 days after Senate receipt: Potter Stewart in 1959 (93 days); Robert H. Bork in 1987 (91 days), Abe Fortas, to be Chief Justice, in 1968 (83 days); and Clarence Thomas in 1991 (81 days).

[42] All of the 15 aforementioned nominations on which the Judiciary Committee voted three days or less after Senate receipt were made prior to 1946, and 14 of the 15 were made prior to 1911.

[43] See bottom rows of Table 1 for median number of days that elapsed from the date Supreme Court nominations were received in the Senate to final Senate vote dates, for three different time spans.

[44] For four Eisenhower nominations, the number of days elapsing from the date received in the Senate to the date voted on by the Senate Judiciary Committee were the following: Earl Warren to be Chief Justice in 1954, 44 days; John M. Harlan II in 1955, 59 days; William J. Brennan Jr. in 1957,

49 days; and Potter Stewart in 1959, 93 days. Three of the nominees — Warren, Brennan, and Stewart — were already on the Court as recess appointees, a circumstance that served perhaps to make action on their nominations seem less urgent to the committee than if their seats on the Court had been vacant. Harlan, however, was not a recess appointee at the time of his nomination. See "The Harlan Nomination," *New York Times*, Feb. 25, 1955, p. 20, discussing, according to the editorial, the "inexcusable delay" on the part of the committee in acting on the nomination and the objections to the nomination voiced by a few of the committee's members. (Ultimately, the committee voted 10-4 to report the nomination favorably.)

[45] The days that elapsed from the date received in the Senate to the date voted on by the Senate Judiciary Committee were eight days and 25 days for the 1962 nominations of Byron R. White and Arthur J. Goldberg and 13 days for the 1965 nomination of Abe Fortas to be Associate Justice.

[46] Besides nominations that received official final Senate action in the form of confirmation or rejection (121 and 11 respectively), or that were withdrawn by the President (11), six others are treated in the table as also receiving final action, albeit not of a definitive official sort — with three having been postponed by the Senate, two tabled, and one (the nomination of Jeremiah S. Black in 1861) not considered after a motion to proceed was defeated by a 25-26 vote. While the six nominations remained pending in the Senate after the noted actions, the effect of the actions, it can be argued, was decisive in eliminating any prospect of confirmation, and thus constituted a final Senate action for time measurement purposes. Accordingly, for these six nominations, the number of days elapsed is measured from date of Senate receipt to the dates of effective final action just noted.

[47] At first glance, the most recently confirmed nomination, of John G. Roberts Jr. for Chief Justice, appears to be a deviation from the 1967 to 2005 median interval from date received to final action of 67 days, as the nomination was confirmed only 23 days after its initial receipt in the Senate. However, it can be argued that a more meaningful context is to see the Roberts Chief Justice nomination (received in the Senate on Sept. 6, 2005) in relation to the earlier July 29, 2005, nomination of Judge Roberts to be Associate Justice. After the death of Chief Justice William H. Rehnquist on Sept. 3, 2005, the Roberts Associate Justice nomination was withdrawn, and he was re-nominated to be Chief Justice. Hearings on the Roberts Associate Justice nomination, set to begin on Sept. 6, were cancelled, and rescheduled hearings, on the Chief Justice nomination, began on Sept. 12. The overall time that elapsed from the Associate Justice nomination of Judge Roberts on

July 29 until Senate confirmation of his Chief Justice nomination on Sept. 29 was 62 days.

[48] Table 1 shows that 43 nominations received final Senate or presidential action three days or less after date of receipt in the Senate. Thirty-six of the 43 were pre-20th century nominations.

[49] Table 1 shows that 15 nominations received final Senate or presidential action more than 75 days after date of receipt in the Senate. Eleven of the 15 were 20th century nominations, with nine made since 1967.

[50] See in Table 1 the recess appointments of Thomas Johnson in 1791, John Rutledge (to be Chief Justice) in 1795, Bushrod Washington in 1798, H. Brockholst Livingston in 1806, Smith Thompson in 1823, John McKinley in 1837, Levi Woodbury in 1845, Benjamin R. Curtis in 1851, and David Davis in 1862.

[51] See in Table 1 the recess appointments of Earl Warren (to be Chief Justice) in 1953, William J. Brennan Jr. in 1956, and Potter Stewart in 1958.

[52] Specifically, Article II, Section 2, clause 3 of the U.S. Constitution empowers the President "to fill up all Vacancies that may happen during the Recess of the Senate, by granting Commissions which shall expire at the End of their next Session."

[53] For background on the history of recess appointments to the Supreme Court, and the policy and constitutional issues associated with those appointments, see CRS Report RL31112, *Recess Appointments of Federal Judges,* by Louis Fisher; and Henry B. Hogue, "The Law: Recess Appointments to Article III Courts," *Political Science Quarterly,* vol. 34, September 2004, p. 656.

Chapter 2

SPEED OF PRESIDENTIAL AND SENATE ACTIONS ON SUPREME COURT NOMINATIONS, 1900-2005*

R. Sam Garrett and Denis Steven Rutkus

ABSTRACT

The speed with which appointments to the Supreme Court move through various stages in the nomination-and-confirmation process is often of great interest to all parties directly involved and the nation as a whole. Shortly after President George W. Bush's October 3, 2005, announcement of White House Counsel Harriet E. Miers as his nominee to replace Associate Justice Sandra Day O'Connor on the Court, both the President and the majority leader of the Senate advocated that the Senate should vote on her nomination "by Thanksgiving" (i.e., within 52 days of the announcement). Senate Judiciary Committee Chairman Arlen Specter stated that he would like to see confirmation hearings on the nomination concluded by Thanksgiving.

This report provides information on the amount of time taken to act on all Supreme Court nominations occurring between 1900 and the present. It focuses on the *actual* amounts of time that Presidents and the Senate have taken to act (as opposed to the elapsed time between *official* points in the process). For example, rather than starting the nomination clock with the official notification of the President of a forthcoming vacancy (e.g., via receipt of a formal retirement letter), this report focuses on when the

* Excerpted from CRS Report RL33118, dated October 18, 2005.

President first *learned* of a Justice's intention to leave the Court (e.g., via a private conversation with the outgoing Justice), or received word that a sitting Justice had died. Likewise, rather than starting the confirmation clock with the transmission of the official nomination to the Senate, this report focuses on when the Senate *became aware* of the President's selection (e.g., via a public announcement by the President).

The data indicate that the entire nomination-and-confirmation process (from when the President first learned of a vacancy to final Senate action) has generally taken almost twice as long for nominees after 1980 than for nominees in the previous 80 years. From 1900 to 1980, the entire process took a median of 59 days; from 1981 through 2005, the process took a median of 113 days. Although Presidents after 1980 have moved more quickly than their predecessors in announcing nominees after learning of vacancies (a median of 18 days compared with 34 days before 1980), the Senate portion of the process (i.e., from the nomination announcement to final Senate action) now appears to take much longer than before (a median of 84 days from 1981 through 2005, compared with 28 days from 1900 through 1980). Most notably, the amount of time between the nomination announcement and first Judiciary Committee hearing has more than tripled — from a median of 13 days (1900-1980) to 51 days (1981-2005). These data suggest that, if recent past experience is a guide, it may be difficult for the Senate to complete action on the Miers nomination by Thanksgiving. However, there is substantial variation within these summary statistics; every nomination has its own pace. For example, Senate consideration of the nomination of Ruth Bader Ginsberg in 1993 took 50 days after the presidential announcement. If the Miers nomination followed that pace, Senate action could be completed by Thanksgiving.

INTRODUCTION

The nomination and confirmation of a Chief Justice or an Associate Justice to the U.S. Supreme Court is an infrequent event of major significance in American public life.[1] To receive what may be lifetime appointment to the Court, a candidate must first be nominated by the President and then confirmed by the Senate. Midway in the appointment process, intensive hearings on a Supreme Court nomination, often taking at least three or four days, are routinely held by the Senate Judiciary Committee, which then can vote on whether to report the nomination to the Senate with a favorable recommendation.

Nominating and confirming Supreme Court Justices is an interdependent process. Neither the President nor the Senate acts alone. The decisions that each branch makes determine how quickly nominations are made and considered, and whether the nomination is successful. This report provides information on the pace of all Supreme Court nominations and confirmations since 1900, focusing on the *actual* amounts of time that Presidents and the Senate have taken to act (as opposed to the elapsed time between *official* points in the process). Events during the summer and fall of 2005 underscored concerns about the speed with which the President makes Supreme Court nominations and the Senate acts on those nominations.

The Roberts Nomination

On July 1, 2005, Associate Justice Sandra Day O'Connor surprised many in official Washington, and possibly President George W. Bush, with a one-paragraph letter announcing her retirement from the Supreme Court, effective upon the confirmation of her successor.[2] Her announcement created the first vacancy on the Court in 11 years. The Court had just concluded its 2004-2005 term, and the opening session of the Court's next term, on October 3, 2005, was three months away. Finding a new Associate Justice took on added urgency, given the failing health of then-Chief Justice William H. Rehnquist. Departure of the Chief Justice as well as Justice O'Connor could result in the need for two Court appointments, and create the possibility of at least one vacancy on the Court when it reconvened in October — unless the new appointments were made expeditiously.

Hours after Justice O'Connor announced her retirement, a senior aide to Senate Majority Leader Bill Frist told reporters that, "Our goal is to have the court back at full strength by the first Monday in October." Senate Judiciary Committee staff were reportedly "poised to begin reviewing background materials" on potential nominees.[3] Nevertheless, appointment of a new Justice in time for the Court's opening session seemed like a challenging goal. In recent years, the Senate Judiciary Committee, and the full Senate as well, had been embroiled in controversies over some of the President's nominations to the lower federal courts. Continued controversy seemed likely surrounding any future nominations to the Supreme Court.

On July 19, 2005, 18 days after receiving Justice O'Connor's retirement letter, President Bush announced his selection of John G. Roberts, Jr., a federal appellate judge, to be the next Associate Justice. Ten days later, on July 29, the President formally nominated Judge Roberts to the Court, with the nomination document immediately transmitted to the Senate, where it was referred to the

Senate Judiciary Committee. Hearings on this nomination were scheduled to begin September 6, but those hearings would never take place.

When Chief Justice William H. Rehnquist died on September 3, Judge Roberts became the first Supreme Court nominee to be withdrawn by the President for one seat on the Court and re-nominated for another. The Senate Judiciary Committee quickly cancelled its Associate Justice hearings, and began Roberts's Chief Justice hearings on September 12, 2005. After receiving a favorable 13-5 vote by the Judiciary Committee on September 22, the nomination of Judge Roberts to be Chief Justice was confirmed by the Senate on the morning of September 29, 2005, by a 78-22 vote. Later that day, the confirmed nominee took both his constitutional and judicial oaths of office at the White House.

Due to the speed with which Judge Roberts was nominated to be Chief Justice and considered by the Senate Judiciary Committee and the full Senate, his appointment was completed in time for the Court to be at full strength at the start of its 2005-2006 term. With the start of that term, Justice O'Connor remained on the Court, in keeping with the intention stated in her retirement letter of stepping down only upon the confirmation of her successor. For his part, President Bush had declined to name a replacement for John Roberts to succeed Sandra Day O'Connor prior to the Senate vote on September 29 confirming Judge Roberts as Chief Justice.

The Miers Nomination

On October 3, 2005, President Bush announced his nomination of White House Counsel Harriet E. Miers to succeed Sandra Day O'Connor as Associate Justice on the Supreme Court. The President said that the Senate had shown during the confirmation of Chief Justice Roberts that it could act promptly, and called upon the Senate to "review [Ms. Miers's] qualifications thoroughly and fairly and to vote on her nomination promptly."[4] At a press conference the next day, the President said that he expected the Senate "to hold an up-or-down vote on Harriet's nomination by Thanksgiving" (i.e., by Nov. 24, 2005).[5] Similarly, Senate Majority Leader Bill Frist called on his colleagues to move "expeditiously but carefully," and encouraged a floor vote "by Thanksgiving."[6] Several news reports suggested that confirmation hearings could begin as early as November 7, 2005. Senator Arlen Specter, Chairman of the Senate Judiciary Committee, reportedly told reporters that he hoped the committee would complete hearings by Thanksgiving[7], but also reportedly emphasized that "thoroughness will be the objective," as opposed to meeting a particular timetable.[8] He also reportedly said that the timing of hearings on the nomination would in part be up to Ms. Miers, who would have to study "so that she would have the grasp of these very complex decisions."[9]

MEASURING THE PACE OF SUPREME COURT APPOINTMENTS

For many Supreme Court appointments, the timing of individual events is determined by the decisions of various key players — by sitting Justices planning to leave the Court; by the President, who selects nominees to fill Court vacancies; and by Senate committee and party leaders, who respectively schedule committee and floor action on Supreme Court nominations. First, Justices who retire or resign from the Court must decide whether to provide the President with advance notice of that decision. For example, Justice Harry A. Blackmun told President William J. Clinton of his decision to retire in 1994, more than four months before the decision became public on April 6 of that year.[10] Justice O'Connor, on the other hand, did not appear to have given President George W. Bush any advance notice when she resigned on July 1, 2005. Also, the mode of presidential notification varies. While President Clinton learned of Justice Blackmun's plans to retire through an informal conversation, Justice O'Connor apparently notified President Bush of her decision through a formal letter.

Once the President chooses a nominee, he alerts the Senate — by public announcement as well as by formal transmission of a written nomination to the Senate. Frequently, the President will announce and formally nominate his Supreme Court choice on the same day, or take both actions within a few days of each other. Less commonly, Presidents announce their intention to nominate a candidate, then make the official nomination a week or more later. The most extreme case of the latter involved President Ronald Reagan in 1981. On July 7 of that year, President Reagan announced he would send the nomination of Sandra Day O'Connor, then an Arizona state appeals court judge, to the Senate "upon completion of all the necessary checks by the Federal Bureau of Investigation."[11] However, it wasn't until almost six weeks later, on August 19, that Judge O'Connor was officially nominated.[12] As noted above, after the Senate receives a Supreme Court nomination, the Judiciary Committee normally holds hearings, followed by final committee action, and consideration before the full chamber.

Official and Unofficial Timetables

The measurement of how long the President and the Senate take to execute their *official* duties surrounding Supreme Court nominations necessarily focuses on official dates of action taken. The most important of these action dates include those on which (1) an outgoing Justice officially informs the President of the intention to step down from the Court (or, alternatively, the date on which a Court seat is vacated due to the death of a Justice), (2) a President formally nominates someone to the Court, the Senate receives the President's nomination, and the nomination is referred to the Senate Judiciary Committee (almost always all on the same date),[13] (3) the Senate Judiciary Committee holds hearings on the nomination, (4) the committee votes on the nomination, and (5) the Senate votes on whether to confirm, or chooses to take no action.

In addition to these dates, however, the President and the Senate usually consider Supreme Court nominations outside official timetables. Just as the President can begin considering a new nominee as soon as he knows a vacancy will arise, the Senate can begin preparing to consider a nominee as soon as the President announces his choice, even if the receipt of the formal nomination is still days or weeks away. Fundamentally, nominations and confirmations to the Supreme Court involve both formal and informal decisions. While formal decisions are easily accessible in historical records, informal decisions — sparsely mentioned in the formal record, or not mentioned at all — might, in many cases, provide better insight into how long the process truly takes.

Objectives of this Report

This report explores the speed of presidential and Senate decision-making surrounding nominations to the Supreme Court from 1900 to the present. During this period, there were a total of 60 vacancies and 66 nominees to the Court.[14] The analysis concentrates on the period 1900-2005 for two primary reasons: (1) relevant historical data for this period are much more readily available and reliable than for earlier Court appointments,[15] and (2) public confirmation hearings for Supreme Court nominations before the Senate Judiciary Committee — an important phase in the Supreme Court appointment process, and one of particular interest to this report — were unheard of before the 20th century.[16]

Although research on Supreme Court nominations often focuses on either presidential or Senate decision-making, this analysis considers the time *both* institutions take to make decisions about, and act on, nominees. The report also takes a unique approach in discussing — as well as can be determined — how long Presidents *actually* take to decide who their nominees will be, and how long the Senate *actually* takes to act on nominations. For example, rather than starting the nomination clock with the official notification of the President of a forthcoming vacancy (e.g., the receipt of a formal retirement letter), this analysis focuses on when the President first *learned* of the vacancy (e.g., a private conversation with the outgoing Justice). Likewise, rather than starting the confirmation clock with the transmission the official nomination to the Senate, this analysis focuses on when the Senate became aware of the President's selection (e.g., by a public announcement by the President).

In many cases, establishing precisely when a President knew that he would have the opportunity to make a Supreme Court nomination is an impossible task. Such information might never have been recorded or known by anyone except the President and his inner circle. However, historical research reveals several instances when a President had advance knowledge of an impending vacancy, well before the public announcement of a Justice's intention to leave the Court. Data sources used to determine when Presidents first knew of vacancies included historical newspapers, official documents such as public presidential papers (which contain Justices' retirement letters to various Presidents), and CRS consultations with presidential libraries.[17] Dates cited throughout this report and in Tables 1-3, at the end of the report, are based on that research.

HOW SUPREME COURT VACANCIES OCCUR

The need for a new appointment to the Court arises when a Justice position becomes vacant, due to death, retirement, or resignation, or when a Justice announces his intention to retire or resign. If the vacated seat is that of the Chief Justice, the President, if he chooses, may nominate a sitting Associate Justice to be Chief, thus setting the stage for the creation of an Associate Justice vacancy as well. Vacancies on the Court also will occur if Justices resign to receive new government appointments or to seek new government positions. When a nomination fails in the Senate, the President must select a new nominee (unless the President chooses to renominate his first choice).

Death of a Sitting Justice

Supreme Court Justices receive what may be lifetime appointments, "good Behaviour" being the only constitutionally specified requirement for continued service.[18] Lifetime tenure, interesting work, and the prestige of the office result in Justices often choosing to serve as long as possible. Historically, a number of Justices have died in office. Most recently, Chief Justice William H. Rehnquist died on September 3, 2005, after battling thyroid cancer for almost a year. Death in office was common on the Court during the first half of the 20th century — 14 of 34 vacancies between 1900-1950. In fact, all five Court vacancies occurring between 1946 and 1954 were due to death of a sitting Justice (see Table 1). Of the 23 vacancies since 1954, though, no Justice had died while still on the Court until Chief Justice Rehnquist in 2005.

Retirement or Resignation of a Sitting Justice

Since 1954, retirement has been by far the most common way in which Justices have left the bench (19 of 23 vacancies occurring after 1954 resulted from retirements). Resignation (i.e., leaving the bench before becoming eligible for retirement compensation) is rare.[19]

In recent history, two Justices have resigned from the Court. Justice Arthur Goldberg resigned in 1965 to assume the post of U.S. Ambassador to the United Nations.[20] Justice Abe Fortas resigned in 1969 after protracted criticism over controversial consulting work while on the bench and a failed nomination to be elevated from Associate Justice to Chief Justice.[21] When Justices retire or resign, the President is usually notified by formal letter. As noted previously, there is evidence in a few cases that a President informally learned of a forthcoming retirement in advance.

Pursuant to a law enacted in 1939, a Justice (or any other federal judge receiving lifetime appointment) may also retire if "unable because of permanent disability to perform the duties of his office," by furnishing the President a certificate of disability.[22] Prior to 1939, specific legislation from Congress was required to provide retirement benefits to a Justice departing the Court because of disability who otherwise would be ineligible for such benefits, due to insufficient age and length of service. In such circumstances in 1910, for instance, Congress took legislative action granting a pension to Justice William H. Moody. As the *Washington Post* reported at the time, although illness had kept Justice Moody from the bench for "almost a year," he was not yet eligible for retirement.[23]

Nomination of a Sitting Justice to Another Position

When a Chief Justice vacancy arises, the President may choose to nominate a sitting Associate Justice for the Court's top post. If the Chief Justice nominee is confirmed, he or she must, to assume the new position, resign as Associate Justice, requiring a new nominee from the President to fill the newly vacated Associate Justice seat.

However, this scenario is relatively rare. During the 1900-2005 period, Presidents attempted to elevate Associate Justices to Chief Justice four times, with the Senate confirming three nominees. Most recently, in 1986, President Ronald Reagan nominated then-Associate Justice William H. Rehnquist to be Chief Justice.[24]

Presidents may also nominate sitting Justices to other political posts, which (if accepted) require resignation from the Court. Between 1900 and 2005, three Justices resigned to pursue other formal public service. In 1916, Justice Charles Evans Hughes resigned to pursue the Republican nomination for President.[25] Justice James F. Byrnes resigned on October 3, 1942, becoming Director of Economic Stability for President Franklin D. Roosevelt.[26] As noted previously, Justice Arthur Goldberg resigned in 1965 to become the U.N. Ambassador.

Controversial, Withdrawn, and Rejected Nominations

When any Court nomination (whether for an Associate or Chief Justice seat) fails in the Senate, the President must either re-submit the nomination or choose another candidate to fill the bench. The entire process thus begins anew. Withdrawals and rejections can greatly increase the amount of time taken to confirm Justices to the Court. Controversial nominees who are eventually confirmed also usually take more time to consider. The late 1960s and early 1970s were one of the most tumultuous periods of nominations and rejections in the Court's history. On May 14, 1969, Justice Abe Fortas resigned from the bench. Fortas had been embroiled in a scandal surrounding his consulting income, and failed to win confirmation as Chief Justice when President Johnson nominated him to the seat in 1968.[27] The Senate rejected President Richard M. Nixon's first two nominees to the Fortas seat — Clement F. Haynsworth, Jr. and G. Harrold Carswell.[28] President Nixon's third choice, Harry A. Blackmun, was not confirmed until May 12, 1970 — almost a year after Fortas's resignation.

Data Presentation

Table 1 (at the end of this report) lists dates for the following events regarding each nomination to the Supreme Court since 1900: (1) when the actual or prospective vacancy apparently became known to the President, (2) when the President announced the nominee, (3) when the Senate Judiciary Committee held its first hearing on the nominee, (4) when final committee action took place, and (5) when final Senate action took place. Table 2 presents the number of days elapsed for five related time intervals: (1) from when the President apparently learned of the actual or prospective vacancy to the his announcement of a new nominee, (2) from the nomination announcement to the first Judiciary Committee hearing, (3) from the first hearing to the committee's final action, (4) from the committee's final action to the Senate's final action, and (5) from the vacancy starting date to final Senate action. Table 3 provides summary statistics for the number of days elapsed during each of these intervals, in addition to the duration of total Senate action, for all nominations from 1900 through 2005, and for two periods within those dates — 1900-1980 and 1981-2005.[29] As discussed later in this report, those periods were chosen because the data indicate a sharp difference in the pace of most nominations before and after 1980.

Date of Actual or Prospective Vacancy

As noted previously, it is often difficult or impossible to determine the specific date that a President first knew he would have the opportunity to name a new Justice to the Supreme Court. The President always has the constitutional obligation to make nominations to the Court when vacancies arise, and is certainly aware of the possibility that vacancies could arise at any time. However, the "Actual or Prospective Vacancy Became Known to President" columns in Tables 1 and 2 focus on documented, specific instances when the President knew he had, or soon would have, the opportunity to name a new Justice to the Court.[30] These dates are based on extensive research about when the Justice's impending departure (or death) was made public, and whether the President had advance knowledge of the vacancy before it became public. In cases in which there is no evidence that the President had advance notice (or in which the data are inconclusive), the date of the first public account of the vacancy marks the beginning of the process (the "When" column in Tables 1 and 2).[31]

For example, Justice Sandra Day O'Connor announced her retirement, pending confirmation of a successor, on July 1, 2005. There is no evidence that

President George W. Bush definitely knew that O'Connor would retire until her announcement. Therefore, July 1, 2005, is used as the starting point for what became the John G. Roberts Associate Justice nomination.[32] On the other hand, although Chief Justice Warren Burger's retirement letter to Ronald Reagan was not released until June 17, 1986, President Reagan's public papers reveal that Burger informed the President of his decision to retire on May 27, 1986.[33] Therefore, May 27, 1986, is used as the starting point for what became the William H. Rehnquist elevation to Chief Justice. Notes throughout Tables 1 and 2 provide information on historical context.

Announcement-of-Nominee Date

Unless otherwise noted, the "President's Announcement-of-Nominee" date in Table 1 is the day when the President announced his nomination to the public or released the text of his nomination letter (whichever came first). This date is significant because it marks the Senate's first opportunity to begin considering the nomination, even if informally. There are a few cases, explained by table notes, in which Presidents announced their decisions less formally, but still publicly. For example, President Harry S. Truman casually told reporters during a July 28, 1949, press conference that he had offered an Associate Justice nomination to then-Attorney General Thomas C. Clark, even though Clark had not yet accepted the nomination.[34] As discussed previously, in some cases, the announcement date differs by days or even weeks from the date the nomination was formally submitted to the Senate.

Use of Medians to Summarize Intervals

Table 2 provides the duration of each major interval in the process of nominating and considering Supreme Court Justices.[35] Table 3 provides the *median* number of days for each major interval in the process. The median is the middle number in a set of observations (in this case, the number of days involved in each stage of considering Supreme Court nominations). The median is generally the preferred measure of central tendency in social science research.[36] As statistician William H. Greene notes, "Loosely speaking, the median corresponds more closely than the mean to the middle of a distribution [group of numbers]. It is unaffected by extreme values."[37] In other words, the median represents the best example of the "average" case, regardless of extremely short or long individual confirmations.

However, in describing the speed of the Supreme Court nomination-and-confirmation process, even median values should be considered carefully. Each nomination is different, and political context and historical factors can have a major impact on when various events occur. Several factors affecting individual nominations to the Court are discussed later in this report.

The Duration of the Nomination-and-Confirmation Process

During the entire period covered by this report (1900-2005), the President and the Senate have each taken varying amounts of time to act on Supreme Court nominations and confirmations. As Table 3 shows, from 1900-2005, Presidents took a median of 29 days after a vacancy occurred to announce their nominees, compared with a median of 50 days for final Senate action once the nomination was announced. The entire process, from actual or prospective vacancy to final Senate action, lasted a median of 74 days from 1900-2005.

However, the amount of time involved in each stage of the nomination-and-confirmation process varies widely when individual cases are examined. Some Supreme Court nominations are unusually fast, coming immediately on the heels a sitting Justice's departure from the bench. In these cases, the President almost certainly knew in advance of the outgoing Justice's intention to retire yet delayed announcement of the retirement to coincide with announcing a new nominee. For example, on May 27, 1986, President Reagan simultaneously announced the retirement of Chief Justice Warren Burger, the elevation of William H. Rehnquist to Chief Justice, and the nomination of Antonin Scalia to assume the Associate Justice seat being vacated by Justice Rehnquist.[38] On the other hand, some nomination decisions can take months — at least to become public. For example, although Justice Harold H. Burton submitted his retirement letter to President Dwight D. Eisenhower on October 6, 1958, Eisenhower did not publicly announce Potter Stewart's nomination until January 17, 1959 — 103 days after announcing Justice Burton's retirement. The entire interval between Burton's announced retirement and Stewart's confirmation lasted 211 days, the bulk of the interval due to a long congressional recess.[39]

Changes During the Past 25 Years

The data indicate that the median decision-making intervals surrounding Supreme Court nominations have changed substantially in the last 25 years.[40] When comparing Supreme Court nominations from 1900-1980 with those from 1981-2005, five patterns stand out. First, after apparently learning of vacancies, Presidents have typically been quicker to announce nominees since 1981 than in the previous 80 years. As shown in Figure 1 (and Table 3), from 1900-1980, Presidents took a median of 34 days to announce their nominees after apparently learning of vacancies, compared with only 18 days from 1981-2005.

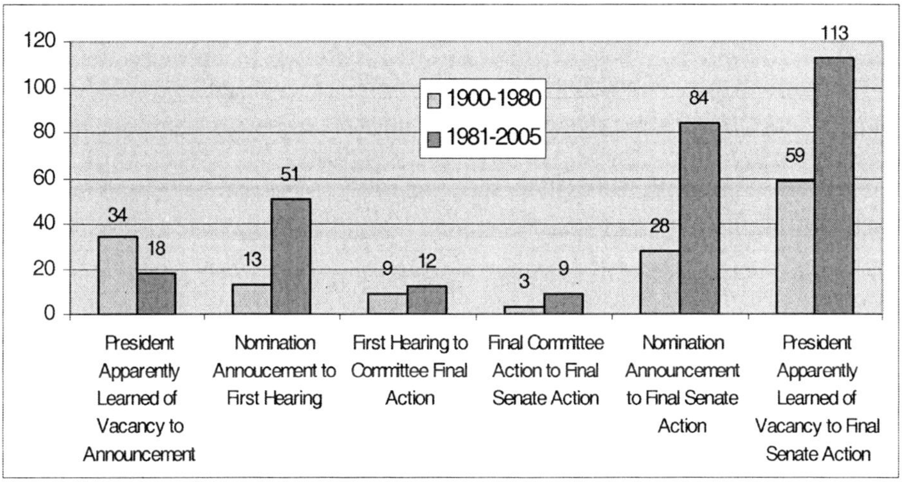

Source: Computations based on data compiled by the CRS authors. Some numbers are rounded. See Table 3 for details.

Figure 1. Speed in Days of Intervals Surrounding Supreme Court Nominations and Confirmations

Second, and perhaps most notably, the median interval between the President's announcement of his nominee and the first Judiciary Committee hearing was substantially longer from 1981-2005 than from 1900-1980. As shown in Figure 1 (and Table 3), this period more than tripled — from 13 days during the 1900-1980 period to 51 days from 1981-2005. Again, however, context is important. Even before hearings begin, the Senate can be actively working on the nomination. For example, prior to the start of John G. Roberts's hearings (and even before his nomination was submitted to the Senate), Senators met privately with Judge Roberts, and some pressed the White House to release records from

Roberts's Department of Justice service.[41] The Harriet Miers nomination has followed a similar pattern. Senators began meeting with Ms. Miers the same day President Bush announced her nomination.

Third, committee and floor action from 1981-2005 also took slightly longer than prior to 1981. From 1981-2005, the Judiciary Committee took a median of 12 days to reach a decision after starting hearings, while the interval between final committee action and final Senate action took 9 days (compared with 9 and 3 days respectively from 1900-1980).[42]

Fourth, as shown in Figure 1 (and Table 3), total Senate activity (the interval between the President's announcement of the nominee and final Senate action) increased from a median of 28 days (1900-1980) to 84 days (1981-2005).[43]

Finally, the entire nomination-and-confirmation process took substantially longer after 1980 than during the previous 80 years. The median duration for the entire process (from when the President apparently became aware of a vacancy until the Senate's final action on the nomination) was almost twice as long from 1981-2005 than during 1900-1980 (113 days versus 59 days, respectively).

Factors Influencing the Speed of the Process

Some elements of the decision-making process surrounding the naming and the confirmation or rejection of Supreme Court nominees are known only to Presidents, nominees, and a few select advisors. Other elements are more obvious. Each nomination has its own political context, making each nomination somewhat different. However, several factors appear to be relatively constant in affecting the speed of Supreme Court nominations and Senate decisions.

How the Vacancy Occurs

How quickly the President announces his nominee and how quickly the Senate considers that nomination can depend on how the vacancy occurred. When Justices die unexpectedly, Presidents can be eager to bring the Court back to full strength as soon as possible. On July 19, 1949, for example, Justice Frank Murphy unexpectedly died of a heart attack after a brief illness.[44] President Harry S. Truman announced his nomination of Thomas C. Clark at a press conference 9 days later, on July 28.[45] The Senate also considered the nomination quickly, beginning hearings on August 9. Clark's entire nomination-and-confirmation process lasted just 30 days. A few months later, Sherman Minton was confirmed even faster — in 24 days — after the death of Justice Wiley B. Rutledge. Nonetheless, sudden death does not guarantee that either the President or the Senate will make nomination-and-confirmation decisions quickly. For example, when Justice Rufus W. Peckham died unexpectedly on October 24, 1909, President William Howard Taft waited 50 days to announce a nominee. Once Taft announced his choice, the Senate confirmed Horace H. Lurton seven days later.

Retirements and resignations are often expected, allowing the President time to prepare for his choice even before an official announcement that a sitting Justice will step down. For example, at the time of his retirement, Justice William O. Douglas's health had been so poor and abilities allegedly in such decline that seven of his fellow Justices voted on October 17, 1975, to "effectively strip Douglas of his power" and excluded the aging Justice from deliberations.[46] By the time Justice Douglas officially wrote to President Gerald R. Ford on November 12, 1975, announcing his retirement, the President was prepared to act quickly. He announced the nomination of John Paul Stevens just 16 days later. Congress, too, acted quickly, confirming Stevens 19 days later, on December 17, 1975.

Sometimes, though, even when retirements or resignations come with advance notice, the process moves slowly. For example, Justice Harry A. Blackmun privately told President William J. Clinton around January 1, 1994, that he was planning to leave the Court. Soon afterward, the White House staff began quietly considering replacements.[47] However, President Clinton did not publicly announce Justice Blackmun's retirement until April 6, did not publicly announce Judge Stephen G. Breyer's nomination until May 13, and did not formally nominate Breyer until May 17.[48] The Judiciary Committee began hearings 60 days after the nomination was announced, and the entire process surrounding Breyer's nomination lasted 209 days. However, decisions affecting the nomination were apparently being made even before Blackmun's retirement became public knowledge.

The Senate's Schedule

Congress's schedule, especially whether the Senate is in session at all, plays an important role in how long Supreme Court nominations take to reach a conclusion. In the early 1900s, several vacancies arose during summer recess or election years when Congress was away from the Capitol. In 1910, for example, Congress adjourned on June 25 and did not return until December 5 —a break of more than five months.[49] In the interim, Chief Justice Melville W. Fuller died of a heart attack on July 4.[50] As press coverage noted at the time, although potential nominees were immediately considered, President William Howard Taft waited to formally submit a nomination to the Senate until Congress reconvened.[51] On December 12, five days after the Senate reconvened, President Taft announced and formally submitted to the Senate his nomination of former Senator Edward D. White of Louisiana to be Chief Justice. That same day, without referring the nomination to the Judiciary Committee, the Senate quickly confirmed Senator White.

Three times during the 1950s, President Eisenhower resorted to recess appointments when Justices died or announced their retirement after Congress had already adjourned for the year.[52] In each case, President Eisenhower formally submitted the nomination after the Senate convened the following January. Of the five persons whom he nominated to the Court, three first received recess appointments and served as Justices before being confirmed — Earl Warren (as Chief Justice) in 1953, William Brennan in 1956, and Potter Stewart in 1958. President Eisenhower's recess appointments, however, generated controversy, prompting the Senate in 1960, voting closely along party lines, to pass a resolution expressing opposition to Supreme Court recess appointments in the future.[53]

President Eisenhower's actions were the most recent recess appointments to the Supreme Court, and recess appointments to the lower federal courts also have become relatively rare since the late 1960s. While a President's constitutional power to make judicial recess appointments was upheld by a federal court in 1985,[54] such appointments, when they do occur, may cause controversy, in large part because they bypass the Senate and its "advice and consent" role. Because of the criticisms of judicial recess appointments in recent decades, the long passage of time since the last Supreme Court recess appointment, and the relatively short duration of contemporary Senate recesses (which arguably undercuts the need for recess appointments to the Court), a President in the 21st century might be expected to make a recess appointment to the Supreme Court only under the most unusual of circumstances.[55]

Today, Congress's availability is less of an obstacle to speedy consideration of nominations than in the past. Given Congress's increasingly year-round schedule, extended decision-making is more often the result of waiting for presidential decisions, background investigations of nominees, or preparations for Judiciary Committee hearings.

Committee Involvement and Institutional Customs

Today, it would be highly unusual for the Judiciary Committee not to hold Supreme Court confirmation hearings lasting at least a few days. In the past, however, the Judiciary Committee often handled Supreme Court nominations without holding hearings at all. As Table 1 shows, of the 22 nominees to the Court from 1900 to 1937, only three had Judiciary Committee hearings (Louis D. Brandeis in 1916, Harlan F. Stone in 1925, and John J. Parker in 1930 (whose nomination was eventually rejected)). In contrast, of the 41 nominees after 1937, only three *did not* have hearings.[56] Nominees did not begin regularly testifying at their own hearings until John M. Harlan did so in 1955.[57]

When the Judiciary Committee holds hearings, Senate floor consideration can be pushed back sometimes by weeks or even months. Controversial nominees often spur protracted hearings. For example, the Judiciary Committee spent 19 days considering Justice Louis D. Brandeis's nomination in 1916, and the interval between the start of hearings and final committee action lasted 105 days. The final Senate vote came eight days later. More recently, the Judiciary Committee, after learning of President Ronald Reagan's selection of Robert H. Bork, took 76 days to hold its first day of hearings on the nomination, and then 21 more days to conclude action on the nomination.

Senate custom plays an especially large role when sitting or former Senators are nominated to the Court. The Senate has almost always considered their colleagues' nominations to the Court within days of receiving the nomination, often without committee hearings or floor debate.[58] For example, although President Taft waited five months to nominate Edward D. White (a former Senator from Louisiana) for Chief Justice, the Senate confirmed the nomination with no debate in less than one hour.[59] Since 1900, three sitting Senators — Hugo L. Black of Alabama (1937), James F. Byrnes of South Carolina (1941), and Harold H. Burton of Ohio (1945) —have been nominated to the Court, and all were quickly confirmed.[60] Senators George Sutherland of Utah (1922) and Sherman Minton of Indiana (1949) were nominated to the Court after having concluded their Senate service. Sutherland was confirmed on the same day on which President Warren Harding announced the nomination, and Minton was confirmed in 19 days.

The decades since 1945 have yet to test again the Senate tradition of bypassing the Judiciary Committee when the Supreme Court nominee is a sitting U.S. Senator; no President since then has nominated a sitting Senator. The last *former* Senator to be nominated to the Court, in 1949, was Judge Sherman Minton of Indiana. (After defeat for re-election to the Senate in 1940, he had been appointed by President Franklin D. Roosevelt to a federal appellate court judgeship.) In a break with tradition, the Supreme Court nomination of former Senator Minton was referred to the Judiciary Committee, and Senate confirmation followed the day after the committee approved the nomination.

Controversial Nominations

As noted previously, withdrawn, rejected, or controversial nominations can substantially lengthen the process. In these cases, although Presidents often name nominees fairly quickly, consideration of the nominations can be drawn out in the Senate. During Judge Robert H. Bork's controversial nomination, for example, Senate consideration of Bork lasted more than a month, from the first Judiciary Committee hearing on September 15, 1987, until the Senate's floor vote to reject the nomination on October 23, 1987. The entire process — from President Reagan's announcement of his intention to nominate Bork to Senate rejection — took 119 days.

Controversy can also delay confirmation of nominees who are ultimately successful. Despite a relatively quick nomination-and-confirmation process of 42 days in late 1924 and early 1925 for then-Attorney General Harlan F. Stone, his nomination was temporarily set back when it was recommitted to the Senate Judiciary Committee, apparently because of Stone's investigation as Attorney General of Senator Burton K. Wheeler.[61] More recently, although Judge Clarence Thomas narrowly won confirmation in 1991, nominating and confirming him took 110 days, including a second round of Judiciary Committee hearings surrounding law professor Anita Hill's allegations against Thomas of sexual harassment.

Discussion and Conclusions

Understanding how long the previous Supreme Court nomination-and-confirmation process has taken, and what factors affected that schedule, can provide useful perspective on presidential decision-making and the Senate's preparations for future nominations. While Presidents and supporters of nominees want Justices confirmed quickly, some Senators will continue to emphasize their right to consider nominees carefully and their responsibility to hold sufficient hearings. Against that political backdrop, this report demonstrates that the length of time required to nominate and confirm or reject a nominee varies widely. Even median durations must be interpreted cautiously. The context surrounding each nomination is particularly important in understanding how long the process takes.

Given the advanced ages of some members of the current Court, more vacancies in the near future are widely anticipated. Should those vacancies occur unexpectedly, such as with a sudden retirement or death, the Court could well be operating without a full bench — making the timing of nominations and confirmations even more pressing. In such a scenario, the Senate would likely be under intense pressure to confirm a successor quickly. This report indicates that, from 1900-1980, the President's portion of the process took longer than the Senate's. Since 1981, though, there has been a substantial increase in the median duration between the President's announcement of a nominee and the start of Judiciary Committee hearings. As a result, the Senate's portion of the process has taken longer than the President's.

Prior to 1981, lengthy nomination-and-confirmation processes usually occurred because either the Senate was out of session when a vacancy on the Court arose, or the nomination was controversial. In recent decades, by contrast, slower decision-making has taken place during an era when Congress is in session longer than during the early 20th century.

In the last 25 years, the nomination-and-confirmation process has lasted a median of 113 days — almost twice as long as the 59-day median from 1900-1980. Although the data in Tables 1-3 provide a median measure of the process, political context is an essential backdrop for understanding the numbers. The President and the Senate share decision-making responsibilities for placing new Justices on the Court. Ultimately, the choices each institution makes determine how long nominations and confirmations take.

One possible explanation for the paradox of slower decisions despite more time in session is that, as some critics on both sides of the aisle contend, Supreme Court nominations have become battlegrounds for larger political debates.[62] Another possibility is that the Senate is considering nominations more carefully than in the past, and therefore taking more time to make decisions about nominees. Similarly, the Senate might be using longer decision-making and scrutiny of nominees as a method of counterbalancing presidential power, especially when Senators believe that the President has chosen an unqualified nominee.

Some early 20th century appointments to the Supreme Court were confirmed within days of a vacancy occurring. More recent nominations and confirmations, by contrast, typically have taken several weeks or months. How and when a vacancy occurs, the Senate's schedule, Judiciary Committee involvement, institutional customs, and whether or not the nomination is controversial, all affect the speed with which the President nominates, and the Senate passes judgment, on prospective Justices.

The Miers Nomination

President Bush and the Senate majority leader have called for the Senate to confirm Harriet Miers as the next Associate Justice of the Supreme Court by Thanksgiving — by November 24, 2005, which will be 52 calendar days after her nomination was announced by the President on October 3. Senator Arlen Specter, Chairman of the Senate Judiciary Committee, reportedly also expressed hope for quick action on the Miers nomination, calling for hearings to be concluded before Thanksgiving.

The Senate has acted with that general degree of speed on one Supreme Court nomination (other than the highly unusual circumstances surrounding Chief Justice Roberts's confirmation) during the past 25 years. After President Clinton announced Ruth Bader Ginsburg's nomination to the Court on June 14, 1993, the Judiciary Committee began hearings 36 days later, on July 20, 1993. The entire Senate portion of action on Ginsburg's nomination lasted 50 days (from President Clinton's announcement of the nomination on June 14 until the Senate vote confirming Ginsburg on August 3, 1993). If Harriet Miers's nomination followed a similar path, Judiciary Committee hearings would start around November 8 (36 days after President Bush's October 3 announcement of Ms. Miers's nomination), with final Senate action occurring around November 22, 2005 (50 days after the October 3 announcement of Ms. Miers's nomination).

However, as discussed previously and as shown in Figure 1 (and Table 3), Senate consideration of all Supreme Court nominations since 1980 has generally taken much longer. From 1981-2005, the Judiciary Committee began confirmation hearings a median of 51 days after presidential announcement of the nomination. The median amount of time for total Senate consideration of Supreme Court nominations (from announcement of the nomination to final Senate action) during the period was 84 calendar days.[63] Therefore, if Senate action on the Miers nomination followed the norm of all other nominations during the past 25 years (i.e., final action in 84 calendar days), the Senate would complete its deliberations regarding the nomination on or about December 26, 2005. The Senate usually adjourns by mid-December, but on rare occasions, extends its session into the new year.

Table 1. Major Events in the Supreme Court Nomination-and-Confirmation Process, 1900-2005

Nominating President	Outgoing Justice	Actual or Prospective Vacancy Apparently Became Known to President		President's Announcement of Nominee		Senate Action Dates on Nomination		
		When	How	Nominee	Date	First Hearing	Committee Final Action	Senate Final Action
Theodore Roosevelt	Horace Gray	09/15/1902	Death of outgoing	Oliver Wendell Holmes	12/02/1902	No record of hearing	12/04/1902	12/04/1902
Theodore Roosevelt	George Shiras, Jr.	08/20/1902[a]	Public reports of imminent retirement	William R. Day	01/14/1903[b]	No record of hearing	02/23/1903	02/23/1903
Theodore Roosevelt	Henry B. Brown	03/08/1906[c]	Outgoing Justice notified President of intention to retire[d]	William H. Moody	11/07/1906	No record of hearing	12/10/1906	12/12/1906
William Howard Taft	Rufus W. Peckham	10/24/1909	Death of outgoing Justice	Horace H. Lurton	12/13/1909[e]	No record of hearing	12/16/1909	12/20/1909
William Howard Taft	David J. Brewer	3/28/1910	Death of outgoing Justice	Charles Evans Hughes	4/25/1910	No record of hearing	05/02/1910	05/02/1910

Table 1. Major Events in the Supreme Court Nomination-and-Confirmation Process, 1900-2005 (Continued)

Nominating President	Outgoing Justice	Actual or Prospective Vacancy Apparently Became Known to President		President's Announcement of Nominee		Senate Action Dates on Nomination		
		When	How	Nominee	Date	First Hearing	Committee Final Action	Senate Final Action
William Howard Taft	Melville W. Fuller *Chief Justice*	07/04/1910	Death of outgoing Chief Justice	Edward D. White	12/12/1910	Nomination was not referred to Judiciary Committee		12/12/1910
William Howard Taft	Edward D. White	12/12/1910	Justice Edward D. White nomination to be Chief Justice	Willis Van Devanter	12/12/1910	No record of hearing	12/15/1910	12/15/1910
William Howard Taft	William H. Moody	06/15/1910[f]	Congressional action authorizing retirement	Joseph R. Lamar	12/12/1910	No record of hearing	12/15/1910	12/15/1910
William Howard Taft	John Marshall Harlan	10/14/1911	Death of outgoing Justice	Mahlon Pitney	02/19/1912	No record of hearing	03/04/1912	03/13/1912
Woodrow Wilson	Horace H. Lurton	07/12/1914	Death of outgoing Justice	James C. McReynolds	08/19/1914[g]	No record of hearing	08/24/1914	08/29/1914

Table 1. Major Events in the Supreme Court Nomination-and-Confirmation Process, 1900-2005 (Continued)

Nominating President	Outgoing Justice	Actual or Prospective Vacancy Apparently Became Known to President		President's Announcement of Nominee		Senate Action Dates on Nomination		
		When	How	Nominee	Date	First Hearing	Committee Final Action	Senate Final Action
Woodrow Wilson	Joseph R. Lamar	01/02/1916	Death of outgoing Justice	Louis D. Brandeis	01/28/1916	02/09/1916	05/24/1916	06/01/1916
Woodrow Wilson	Charles Evans Hughes	06/10/1916[h]	Resignation letter submitted to President	John H. Clarke	07/14/1916	No record of hearing	07/24/1916	07/24/1916
Warren Harding	Edward D. White	05/19/1921	Death of outgoing Justice	William Howard Taft	06/30/1921	Nomination was not referred to Judiciary Committee		06/30/1921
Warren Harding	John H. Clarke	09/05/1922	Resignation letter submitted to President	George Sutherland	09/05/1922	Nomination was not referred to Judiciary Committee		09/05/1922

Table 1. Major Events in the Supreme Court Nomination-and-Confirmation Process, 1900-2005 (Continued)

Nominating President	Outgoing Justice	Actual or Prospective Vacancy Apparently Became Known to President		President's Announcement of Nominee		Senate Action Dates on Nomination		
		When	How	Nominee	Date	First Hearing	Committee Final Action	Senate Final Action
Warren Harding	William R. Day	09/05/1922[i]	Public reports of imminent retirement	Pierce Butler	11/23/1922	No record of hearing	11/28/1922	Placed on Executive Calendar on 11/28/1922, with no record of further action[j]
		12/04/1922	Lack of action on first nomination of Butler	Pierce Butler	12/05/1922	No record of hearing	12/18/1922	12/21/1922
Warren Harding	Mahlon Pitney	12/16/1922	White House announced forthcoming retirement[k]	Edward T. Sanford	01/09/1923[l]	No record of hearing	01/29/1923	01/29/1923

Table 1. Major Events in the Supreme Court Nomination-and-Confirmation Process, 1900-2005 (Continued)

Nominating President	Outgoing Justice	Actual or Prospective Vacancy Apparently Became Known to President		President's Announcement of Nominee		Senate Action Dates on Nomination		
		When	How	Nominee	Date	First Hearing	Committee Final Action	Senate Final Action
Calvin Coolidge	Joseph McKenna	12/25/1924[m]	Public reports of forthcoming retirement	Harlan F. Stone	01/05/1925	01/28/1925	01/21/1925	Recommitted 01/26/1925
							02/02/1925	02/05/1925
Herbert Hoover	William Howard Taft *Chief Justice*	02/03/1930	Retirement letter submitted to President	Charles Evans Hughes	02/03/1930	No record of hearing	02/10/1930	02/13/1930
Herbert Hoover	Edward T. Sanford	03/08/1930	Death of outgoing Justice	John J. Parker	03/21/1930	04/05/1930	04/17/1930	Rejected 05/07/1930
Herbert Hoover	Edward T. Sanford	05/07/1930	Parker nomination rejected by Senate	Owen J. Roberts	05/09/1930	No record of hearing	05/19/1930	05/20/1930
Herbert Hoover	Oliver Wendell Holmes, Jr.	01/12/1932	Retirement letter submitted to President	Benjamin N. Cardozo	02/15/1932	No record of hearing	02/23/1932	02/24/1932

Table 1. Major Events in the Supreme Court Nomination-and-Confirmation Process, 1900-2005 (Continued)

Nominating President	Outgoing Justice	Actual or Prospective Vacancy Apparently Became Known to President		President's Announcement of Nominee		Senate Action Dates on Nomination		
		When	How	Nominee	Date	First Hearing	Committee Final Action	Senate Final Action
Franklin D. Roosevelt	Willis Van Devanter	05/18/1937[n]	Retirement letter submitted to President	Hugo L. Black	08/12/1937	No record of hearing	08/16/1937	08/17/1937
Franklin D. Roosevelt	George Sutherland	01/05/1938	Retirement letter submitted to President	Stanley F. Reed	01/15/1938[o]	01/20/1938	01/24/1938	01/25/1938
Franklin D. Roosevelt	Benjamin N. Cardozo	07/09/1938[p]	Death of outgoing Justice	Felix Frankfurter	01/05/1939	01/07/1939	01/16/1939	01/17/1939
Franklin D. Roosevelt	Louis D. Brandeis	02/13/1939[q]	Retirement letter submitted to President	William O. Douglas	03/20/1939	03/24/1939	03/27/1939	04/04/1939
Franklin D. Roosevelt	Pierce Butler	11/16/1939	Death of outgoing Justice	Frank Murphy	01/04/1940	No record of hearing	01/15/1940	01/16/1940

Table 1. Major Events in the Supreme Court Nomination-and-Confirmation Process, 1900-2005 (Continued)

Nominating President	Outgoing Justice	Actual or Prospective Vacancy Apparently Became Known to President		President's Announcement of Nominee		Senate Action Dates on Nomination		
		When	How	Nominee	Date	First Hearing	Committee Final Action	Senate Final Action
Franklin D. Roosevelt	James Clark McReynolds	01/22/1941	Outgoing Justice notified President of intention to retire [r]	James F. Byrnes	06/12/1941	Nomination was not referred to Judiciary Committee		06/12/1941
Franklin D. Roosevelt	Charles Evans Hughes *Chief Justice*	06/02/1941[s]	Retirement letter submitted to President	Harlan F. Stone	06/12/1941	06/21/1941	06/23/1941	06/27/1941
Franklin D. Roosevelt	Harlan F. Stone	06/12/1941	Harlan F. Stone nomination to be Chief Justice	Robert H. Jackson	06/12/1941	06/21/1941	06/30/1941	07/07/1941
Franklin D. Roosevelt	James F. Byrnes	10/03/1942[t]	Byrnes appointment to other public office	Wiley B. Rutledge	01/11/1943	01/22/1943	02/01/1943	02/08/1943

Table 1. Major Events in the Supreme Court Nomination-and-Confirmation Process, 1900-2005 (Continued)

Nominating President	Outgoing Justice	Actual or Prospective Vacancy Apparently Became Known to President		President's Announcement of Nominee		Senate Action Dates on Nomination		
		When	**How**	**Nominee**	**Date**	**First Hearing**	**Committee Final Action**	**Senate Final Action**
Harry S. Truman	Owen J. Roberts	06/30/1945[u]	Retirement letter submitted to President	Harold H. Burton	09/18/1945	No record of hearing	09/19/1945	09/19/1945
Harry S. Truman	Harlan F. Stone *Chief Justice*	04/22/1946	Death of outgoing Chief Justice	Fred M. Vinson	06/06/1946	06/14/1946	06/19/1946	06/20/1946
Harry S. Truman	Frank Murphy	07/19/1949	Death of outgoing Justice	Thomas C. Clark	07/28/1949	08/09/1949	08/12/1949	08/18/1949
Harry S. Truman	Wiley B. Rutledge	09/10/1949	Death of outgoing Justice	Sherman Minton	09/15/1949	09/27/1949	10/03/1949	10/4/1949
Dwight D. Eisenhower	Fred M. Vinson *Chief Justice*	09/08/1953	Death of outgoing Chief Justice	Earl Warren	***Recess appointment, 10/02/1953***			
					01/11/1954	02/02/1954	02/24/1954	03/01/1954

Table 1. Major Events in the Supreme Court Nomination-and-Confirmation Process, 1900-2005 (Continued)

Nominating President	Outgoing Justice	Actual or Prospective Vacancy Apparently Became Known to President		President's Announcement of Nominee		Senate Action Dates on Nomination		
		When	How	Nominee	Date	First Hearing	Committee Final Action	Senate Final Action
Dwight D. Eisenhower	Robert H. Jackson	10/09/1954	Death of outgoing Justice	John Marshall Harlan II	11/08/1954[v]	No record of hearing, committee vote, or Senate vote		
		01/05/1955 (Congress reconvenes)	Lack of action on first nomination of Harlan nomination	John Marshall Harlan II	01/10/1955	02/24/1955	03/10/1955	03/16/1955
Dwight D. Eisenhower	Sherman Mintcn	09/07/1956	Retirement letter submitted to President	William J. Brennan	***Recess appointment, 10/15/1956***			
					01/14/1957	02/27/1957	03/04/1957	03/19/1957
Dwight D. Eisenhower	Stanley F. Reed	01/31/1957	Press conference held by Reed announcing retirement[w]	Charles E. Whittaker	03/02/1957	03/18/1957	03/18/1957	03/19/1957

Table 1. Major Events in the Supreme Court Nomination-and-Confirmation Process, 1900-2005 (Continued)

Nominating President	Outgoing Justice	Actual or Prospective Vacancy Apparently Became Known to President		President's Announcement of Nominee		Senate Action Dates on Nomination		
		When	How	Nominee	Date	First Hearing	Committee Final Action	Senate Final Action
Dwight D. Eisenhower	Harold H. Burton	10/06/1958	Retirement letter submitted to President	Potter Stewart	*Recess Appointment, 10/14/1958*			
					01/17/1959	04/09/1959	04/20/1959	05/05/1959
John F. Kennedy	Charles E. Whittaker	03/28/1962	Retirement letter received by President[x]	Byron R. White	03/30/1962[y]	04/11/1962	04/11/1962	04/11/1962
John F. Kennedy	Felix Frankfurter	08/28/1962[z]	Retirement letter submitted to President	Arthur J. Goldberg	08/29/1962	09/11/1962	09/25/1962	09/25/1962
Lyndon B. Johnson	Arthur J. Goldberg	07/20/1965	Goldberg appointment to other public office[aa]	Abe Fortas	07/28/1965[bb]	08/05/1965	08/10/1965	08/11/1965

Table 1. Major Events in the Supreme Court Nomination-and-Confirmation Process, 1900-2005 (Continued)

Nominating President	Outgoing Justice	Actual or Prospective Vacancy Apparently Became Known to President		President's Announcement of Nominee		Senate Action Dates on Nomination		
		When	How	Nominee	Date	First Hearing	Committee Final Action	Senate Final Action
Lyndon B. Johnson	Thomas C. Clark	02/28/1967	Outgoing Justice notified President of intention to retire[cc]	Thurgood Marshall	06/13/1967[dd]	07/13/1967	08/03/1967	08/30/1967
Lyndon B. Johnson	Earl Warren *Chief Justice*	06/13/1968[ee]	Retirement letter submitted to President	Abe Fortas	06/26/1968	07/11/1968	09/26/1968	10/01/1968 (Cloture motion rejected)
Lyndon B. Johnson	Abe Fortas	06/26/1968[ff]	Fortas nomination to be Chief Justice	Homer Thornberry	06/26/1968	07/11/1968	No record of committee vote	Nomination withdrawn by President, 10/04/1968

Table 1. Major Events in the Supreme Court Nomination-and-Confirmation Process, 1900-2005 (Continued)

Nominating President	Outgoing Justice	Actual or Prospective Vacancy Apparently Became Known to President		President's Announcement of Nominee		Senate Action Dates on Nomination		
		When	How	Nominee	Date	First Hearing	Committee Final Action	Senate Final Action
Richard M. Nixon	Earl Warren *Chief Justice*	01/20/1969[gg]	Fortas Chief Justice nomination withdrawn by President Johnson (10/04/1968)	Warren E. Burger	05/21/1969	06/03/1969	06/03/1969	06/09/1969

Table 1. Major Events in the Supreme Court Nomination-and-Confirmation Process, 1900-2005 (Continued)

Nominating President	Outgoing Justice	Actual or Prospective Vacancy Apparently Became Known to President		President's Announcement of Nominee		Senate Action Dates on Nomination		
		When	How	Nominee	Date	First Hearing	Committee Final Action	Senate Final Action
Richard M. Nixon	Abe Fortas	05/14/1969	Resignation letter submitted to President	Clement F. Haynsworth, Jr.	08/18/1969[hh]	09/16/1969	10/09/1969	11/21/1969 (Rejected)
		11/21/1969	Haynsworth nomination rejected by Senate	G. Harrold Carswell	01/19/1970	01/27/1970	02/16/1970	04/08/1970 (Rejected)
		04/08/1970	Carswell nomination rejected by Senate	Harry A. Blackmun	04/14/1970	04/29/1970	05/06/1970	05/12/1970
Richard M. Nixon	Hugo L. Black	09/17/1971	Retirement letter submitted to President	Lewis F. Powell, Jr.	10/21/1971	11/03/1971	11/23/1971	12/06/1971

Table 1. Major Events in the Supreme Court Nomination-and-Confirmation Process, 1900-2005 (Continued)

Nominating President	Outgoing Justice	Actual or Prospective Vacancy Apparently Became Known to President		President's Announcement of Nominee		Senate Action Dates on Nomination		
		When	How	Nominee	Date	First Hearing	Committee Final Action	Senate Final Action
Richard M. Nixon	John Marshall Harlan II	09/23/1971	Retirement letter submitted to President	William H. Rehnquist	10/21/1971	11/03/1971	11/23/1971	12/10/1971
Gerald R. Ford	William O. Douglas	11/12/1975[ii]	Retirement letter submitted to President	John Paul Stevens	11/28/1975[jj]	12/8/1975	12/11/1975	12/17/1975
Ronald Reagan	Potter Stewart	05/18/1981[kk]	Retirement letter submitted to President	Sandra Day O'Connor	07/07/1981[ll]	09/09/1981	09/15/1981	09/21/1981
Ronald Reagan	Warren E. Burger *Chief Justice*	05/27/1986[mm]	Chief Justice privately alerted President of intention to retire	William H. Rehnquist	06/17/1986	07/29/1986	08/14/1986	09/17/1986

Table 1. Major Events in the Supreme Court Nomination-and-Confirmation Process, 1900-2005 (Continued)

Nominating President	Outgoing Justice	Actual or Prospective Vacancy Apparently Became Known to President		President's Announcement of Nominee		Senate Action Dates on Nomination		
		When	How	Nominee	Date	First Hearing	Committee Final Action	Senate Final Action
Ronald Reagan	William H. Rehnquist	05/27/1986[nn]	Rehnquist nomination by Reagan to be Chief Justice	Antonin Scalia	06/17/1986	08/05/1986	08/14/1986	09/17/1986
Ronald Reagan	Lewis F. Powell, Jr.	06/26/1987[oo]	Press conference held by Powell announcing retirement	Robert H. Bork	07/01/1987	09/15/1987	10/06/1987	10/23/1987 (Rejected)
		10/23/1987	Bork nomination rejected by Senate	Douglas H. Ginsburg	10/29/1987	Ginsburg withdrew (11/07/1987) before official nomination[pp]		
		11/07/1987	Ginsburg withdrawal	Anthony M. Kennedy	11/11/1987	12/14/1987	01/27/1988	02/03/1988

Table 1. Major Events in the Supreme Court Nomination-and-Confirmation Process, 1900-2005 (Continued)

Nominating President	Outgoing Justice	Actual or Prospective Vacancy Apparently Became Known to President		President's Announcement of Nominee		Senate Action Dates on Nomination		
		When	How	Nominee	Date	First Hearing	Committee Final Action	Senate Final Action
George H.W. Bush	William J. Brennan	07/20/1990	Retirement letter submitted to President	David H. Souter	07/23/1990[qq]	09/13/1990	09/27/1990	10/02/1990
George H.W. Bush	Thurgood Marshall	06/27/1991	Retirement letter submitted to President	Clarence Thomas	07/01/1991	09/10/1991	09/27/1991	10/15/1991
William J. Clinton	Byron R. White	03/19/1993[rr]	Retirement letter submitted to President	Ruth Bader Ginsburg	06/14/1993[ss]	07/20/1993	07/29/1993	08/03/1993
William J. Clinton	Harry A. Blackmun	01/01/1994[tt]	Justice privately alerted President of forthcoming retirement	Stephen G. Breyer	05/13/1994	07/12/1994	07/19/1994	07/29/1994

Table 1. Major Events in the Supreme Court Nomination-and-Confirmation Process, 1900-2005 (Continued)

Nominating President	Outgoing Justice	Actual or Prospective Vacancy Apparently Became Known to President		President's Announcement of Nominee		Senate Action Dates on Nomination		
		When	How	Nominee	Date	First Hearing	Committee Final Action	Senate Final Action
George W. Bush	Sandra Day O'Connor	07/01/2005	Retirement letter submitted to President	John G. Roberts	07/19/2005	Nomination withdrawn by President (09/05/2005) re-nominated as Chief Justice (09/05/2005)	Nomination withdrawn by President (09/05/2005), re-nominated as Chief Justice (09/05/2005)	Nomination withdrawn by President (09/05/2005), re-nominated as Chief Justice (09/05/2005)
		09/05/2005	Announcement of Roberts nomination withdrawal and re-submission by President	Harriet E. Miers	10/03/2005			
George W. Bush	William H. Rehnquist	09/03/2005	Death of outgoing Justice	John G. Roberts	09/05/2005	09/12/2005	09/22/2005	09/29/2005

Sources: As described in the text, this research relied on historical newspapers, official presidential papers, and CRS correspondence with Presidential Libraries. Ward's *Deciding to Leave* was especially useful in compiling data on the reasons why Justices left the bench. Additional source information appears in the table notes below.

a. It is unclear when President Theodore Roosevelt learned of Justice Shiras's intention to retire. However, *Washington Post* coverage suggests that Shiras's forthcoming departure was well known in Washington, DC by at least Aug. 20, 1902 ("Knox May Not Want It: Belief that He Would Decline Justice Shiras's Position," *Washington Post*, Aug. 20, 1902, p. 1).

b. President Roosevelt did not formally announce Day's nomination until Feb. 19, 1903. However, the *Washington Post* reported as early as Jan. 14, 1903 that President Roosevelt had already offered Day the nomination, after William Howard Taft declined the offer in favor of continuing his position as Civil Governor of the Philippine Islands ("Declined by Taft," *Washington Post*, Jan. 14, 1903, p. 1).

c. According to the *Washington Post*, Justice Brown notified the President, on Mar. 8, 1906, that he wished to retire ("To Leave the Bench: Justice Brown Will Retire in the Fall," *Washington Post*, Mar. 8, 1906, p. 3).

d. It is unclear from the historical record whether the President learned of Justice Brown's desire to retire by letter, personal conversation, etc.

e. Despite the delay between Justice Peckham's death and President William Howard Taft's nomination of Horace H. Lurton, President Taft, in nominating Lurton, was reportedly "adhering to his original purpose to promote Judge Lurton, whom he has known for years, and with whom he served on the bench," ("Taft Names Lurton," *Washington Post*, Dec. 14, 1909, p. 3).

f. Justice Moody did not actually depart the Court until Nov. 20, 1910 (Ward, *Deciding to Leave*, p. 5). However, "Illness of a serious nature has kept Justice Moody from his duties in the Supreme Court for almost a year. There have been occasional rumors of retirement, but Senator Lodge [on June 15, 1910] presented the real harbinger of that action, in the form of a bill extending the statute relating to retirement from the Supreme Court to cover the case of Mr. Moody" ("Moody Will Retire," *Washington Post*, June 15, 1910, p. 1).

g. Although Justice McReynolds's nomination was not announced until Aug. 20, 1914, the *Washington Post* reported on Aug. 19 that President Woodrow Wilson had "definitely decided" on McReynolds ("Picks M'Reynolds," *Washington Post*, Aug. 19, 1914, p. 1), thereby informally alerting Congress to the President's choice.

h. On June 10, 1916, Justice Hughes resigned to pursue the 1916 Republican presidential nomination ("Hughes, With Words That Ring, Obeys Call to Lead Republicans," *Washington Post*, June 11, 1916, p. 1). Although historical media research does not indicate that President Wilson knew for certain that Justice Hughes would resign, media reports had hinted at a Hughes resignation throughout the spring of 1916.

i. Day did not leave the Court until Nov. 13, 1922. However, the *Washington Post* reported that Day's consideration of retirement was mentioned at a White House briefing on Sept. 5, 1922 ("Justice Day May Leave the Bench," *Washington Post*, Sept. 6, 1922, p. 1).

j. After the Senate took no final action on Butler's nomination by the end of the third session of the 67th Congress on Dec. 4, 1922, President Warren Harding re-nominated Butler on Dec. 5, 1922. See "Fight Over Butler's Nomination Forecast," *Washington Post*, Dec. 6, 1922, p. 12; and "Fight Against Butler Opened by Shipstead," *Washington Post*, Dec. 9, 1922, p. 2.

k. Although Justice Pitney's resignation was effective as of Dec. 31, 1922, the White House announced Pitney's forthcoming departure on Dec. 16, 1922 ("Resigns," *Chicago Daily Tribune*, Dec. 17, 1922, p. 17).

l. President Warren Harding did not officially nominate Sanford until Jan. 24, 1923. However, the media reported as early as Jan. 9, 1923, that President Harding intended to nominate Sanford ("E.T. Sanford Choice for Supreme Court," *Washington Post*, Jan. 9, 1923, p. 1).

m. Justice McKenna did not officially retire until Jan. 5, 1925. However, the media reported his imminent retirement on Dec. 25, 1924 ("M'Kenna to Retire Soon as a Justice of the Supreme Court," *Washington Post*, Dec. 25, 1924, p. 2).

n. For an account of Justice Van Devanter privately alerting a reporter of his decision to retire on the morning of the announcement, see "News 'Beat' Aided by Van Devanter," *New York Times*, May 23, 1937, p. 40.

o. Justice Reed had also been a frontrunner for the 1937 seat that eventually went to Justice Hugo Black. This perhaps explains President Franklin D. Roosevelt's relatively quick nomination of Reed, despite what many reporters considered to be a surprise retirement announcement from Sutherland. See Robert C. Albright, "Sutherland, 75, Quits U.S. Supreme Court," *New York Times*, Jan. 6, 1938, p. X1; and Franklyn Waltman, "Stanley F. Reed Named to U.S. Supreme Court." *New York Times*, Jan. 16, 1938, p. 1.

p. Although Justice Cardozo had been ill and away from the bench since December 1937 (United Press, "Supreme Court Liberal Succumbs to Heart Ailment in N.Y.," *Washington Post*, July 10, 1938, p. M1), a definite need to nominate a new Justice did not occur until Cardozo's death on July 9, 1938.

q. Justice Brandeis had been away from the bench for a month, recovering from a heart attack, prior to announcing his retirement (United Press, "Justice Brandeis, Dean of Supreme Court, Quits," *Los Angeles Times*, Feb. 14, 1939, p. 1). Nonetheless, his retirement was considered abrupt, suggesting that President Roosevelt had little advance notice to consider a successor.

r. It is unclear from the historical record whether the President learned of Justice McReynolds's desire to retire by letter, personal conversation, etc.

s. Although Chief Justice Hughes's retirement due to age and poor health had been "rumored some months" prior to submission of his formal retirement letter (Walter Trohan, "Hughes Retires From Court," *Chicago Daily Tribune*, June 3, 1941, p. 1), the definite need for a new nominee did not arise until Hughes announced his retirement.

t. Justice Byrnes resigned at President Roosevelt's request on Oct. 3, 1942, becoming Director of Economic Stability. Roosevelt was, therefore, aware of an impending vacancy on the Court prior to the formal resignation, although the precise date is unclear. For a summary of Byrnes's transition from the Court to his new post, see Associated Press, "Byrnes Resigns From Bench in Letter to President," *New York Times*, Oct. 4, 1942, p. 45.

u. Although President Truman did not announce Justice Roberts's intention to retire until July 5, 1945 (United Press, "Morganthau and Roberts Resign," *Los Angeles Times*, July 6, 1945, p. 1), Justice Roberts's retirement letter is dated July 30, 1945. Truman received the letter on that date "or soon thereafter" (e-mail communication between CRS Information Specialist Dana Ely and Truman Library Archivist Randy Sowell, Sept. 2, 2005).

v. The Senate took no final action on the Harlan nomination before the 83rd Congress's final adjournment on Dec. 2, 1954. President Eisenhower re-nominated Harlan to the Court on Jan. 10, 1955, five days after the start of the first session of the 84th Congress. Evidence does not suggest that another announcement of the nomination was made.

w. Whether President Eisenhower first learned of Justice Reed's retirement through the press conference or a letter from Reed is unclear. Contemporary media coverage mentioned a press conference and a letter to Eisenhower (Edward T. Folliard, "Reed Is Retiring From High Court," *Washington Post*, Feb. 1, 1957, p. A1). However, political scientist Artemus Ward's account asserts that Reed announced his retirement through a press conference (Ward, *Deciding to Leave*, pp. 162-163). Regardless, both events occurred on Jan. 31, 1957. For the Jan. 31 correspondence between Reed and Eisenhower, see "Letter to Stanley Reed Regarding His Retirement From Active Service as An Associate Justice of the Supreme Court," U.S. National Archives and Records Administration, Office of the Federal Register, *Public Papers of the Presidents of the United States: Dwight D. Eisenhower, 1957* (Washington: GPO, 1958), pp. 109-110.

x. This information is based on e-mail communication between CRS Information Specialist Dana Ely and Kennedy Library Reference Technician Sharon Kelly, Sept. 14, 2005.

y. According to a press account, President Kennedy's decision to nominate White "was apparently made just a few hours before the selection was announced Friday night" (on March 30, 1962) (James E. Clayton, "White Was One of Three In Line for High Court," *Washington Post*, Apr. 1, p. A1). Given the relatively quick action, however, Kennedy might have considered White as a Supreme Court candidate in advance of the Mar. 28, 1962, announced vacancy.

z. Aug. 28, 1962, is the only definitive date which can be established based on available data, as the earliest point at which President Kennedy learned of Justice Frankfurter's intention to retire. However, President Kennedy's quick nomination of Goldberg, and Justice Frankfurter's poor health in the weeks leading up to his retirement, suggest that President Kennedy was considering prospective nominees well before Frankfurter stepped down. Kennedy's letter to Justice Frankfurter accepting his retirement references a visit the President paid to Frankfurter to check on his health sometime during the summer of 1962 (U.S. National Archives and Records Administration, Office of the Federal Register, *Public Papers of the Presidents of the United States: John F. Kennedy, 1962*, (Washington: GPO, 1963), p. 656). According to Kennedy Library Reference Technician Sharon Kelly, Kennedy's office files suggest that correspondence between Frankfurter, Special Assistant for National Security Affairs McGeorge Bundy, and the President would have alerted Kennedy to Frankfurter's declining health around May 17, 1962 (e-mail communication between CRS Information Specialist Dana Ely and Kennedy Library Reference Technician Sharon Kelly, Sept. 14, 2005).

aa. President Lyndon B. Johnson unexpectedly nominated Justice Goldberg to be U.S. Ambassador to the United Nations following the death on July 14, 1965, of the previous ambassador, Adlai E. Stevenson. See Carroll Kilpatrick, "Goldberg is Named to Stevenson Post," *Washington Post*, July 21, 1965, p. A1.

bb. Although Justice Fortas was not nominated until July 28, 1965, President Johnson apparently decided to nominate Fortas long before the Goldberg vacancy, making the gap of only one week between Goldberg's resignation and Fortas's nomination unsurprising. At the press conference announcing Fortas's nomination, President Johnson said that he and Fortas had discussed the nomination "on numerous occasions in the 20 months," (U.S. National Archives and Records Administration, Office of the Federal Register, *Public Papers of the Presidents of the United States: Lyndon B. Johnson, 1966*, vol. 2 (Washington: GPO), 1967, p. 798).

cc. Despite the fact that Justice Clark announced his forthcoming retirement on Feb. 28, 1967, historical evidence suggests that Johnson might have prompted Clark's retirement as early as Jan. 1967, when the President prepared to nominated Justice Clark's son, Ramsey, to be Attorney General. "On January 25, 1967, Johnson told Ramsey that he could only be named the permanent attorney general if his father stepped down from the Court" (Ward, *Deciding to Leave*, p. 170).

dd. Like the 1965 Fortas nomination, Marshall's nomination was no surprise, since Johnson was reportedly considering Marshall for appointment to the Court before the formal nomination. According to a 1967 *Washington Post* report, "Marshall's resignation two years ago, at the President's request, from a lifetime seat on the 2d U.S. Circuit Court of Appeals to become Solicitor General, had seemed clearly a move to groom him for the Nation's highest court" (John P. MacKenzie, "LBJ Names Marshall to Court," June 14], 1967, *Washington Post*, p. A1).

ee. Although President Johnson did not announce Chief Justice Warren's retirement until June 26, he received Warren's retirement letter on June 13, 1968 (U.S. National Archives and Records Administration, Office of the Federal Register, *Public Papers of the Presidents of the United States: Lyndon B. Johnson, 1968-69*, vol. 1 (Washington: GPO), 1970, p. 746).

ff. Although a specific opportunity to name a new Associate Justice did not arise until the Fortas Chief Justice nomination on June 26, 1968, it was reported that "[s]ome Texans at the Capitol are sure that Mr. Johnson has planned for the last four years to name Thornberry to the Supreme Court before he [Johnson] left office," (Richard L. Lyons, "Homer Thornberry: 'Constructive Liberal,' Close LBJ friend," *Washington Post,* June 27, 1969, p. 1).

gg. Jan. 20, 1969 (the date of Richard M. Nixon's inauguration), is used as the starting date for the vacancy because it marks the beginning of President Nixon's official decision-making powers. After the Abe Fortas Chief Justice nomination failed, President Johnson announced on Oct. 2, 1968, that he would not name another nominee (U.S. National Archives and Records Administration, Office of the Federal Register, *Public Papers of the Presidents of the United States: Lyndon B. Johnson, 1968-69*, vol. 2 (Washington: GPO), 1966, p. 509). Eight days later, Johnson elaborated on his decision. The President wrote that although he would have made another nomination in "ordinary times," the situation was extraordinary and that, "Under the circumstances, the foundations of government would be better served by the present Chief Justice [Earl Warren] remaining [in office] until emotionalism subsides, reason and fairness prevail (U.S. National Archives and Records Administration, Office of the Federal Register, *Public Papers of the Presidents of the United States: Lyndon B. Johnson, 1968-69*, vol. 2 (Washington: GPO, 1970), p. 1024). On Dec. 3, 1968, Chief Justice Warren informed President-elect Richard M. Nixon that he was willing to continue serving until a successor was confirmed ("Statement by the Chief Justice," Dec. 4, 1968, Earl Warren Papers, Manuscript Division, Library of Congress, Washington, DC). In a May 1969, conversation with reporters, President Nixon offered an unusually detailed discussion of his decision-making process surrounding the Burger nomination. Nixon reported that he thought "it would not be a proper mark of respect for the Court and for the Chief Justice to have a nomination go down, say, in February or March, and then have possibly the Senate hearings and the like at a time that the Court was sitting," and that his target date for a nomination decision was between May 1 and June 1, 1968 (U.S. National Archives and Records Administration, Office of the Federal Register, *Public Papers of the Presidents of the United States: Richard Nixon, 1970*, (Washington: GPO), 1971, p. 390).

hh. Although President Richard M. Nixon waited until Aug. 18, 1969, to nominate Haynsworth, media accounts speculated that Haynsworth would be the nominee at least as early as Aug. 6. See AP, "Possible High Court Choice Hit," *Washington Post*, Aug. 7, 1969, p. B4.

ii. Chief Justice Warren Burger reportedly "hint[ed] at a possible vacancy" on the Court in a letter to President Gerald Ford on Nov. 10, 1975, and offered "factors for [the President] to consider when appointing a new justice," (e-mail communication between CRS Information Specialist Dana Ely and Ford Library Archivist Technician Joshua Cochran, Sept. 12, 2005). Justice Douglas's health had been in question since Dec. 31, 1974, when he suffered a stroke (John P. MacKenzie, "Douglas Retires From Court," *Washington Post*, Nov. 13, 1975, p. A1). However, President Ford would have had relatively little time to consider a replacement Justice since he did not assume the presidency until Aug. 9, 1975, and a vacancy did not officially arise until Justice Douglas's Nov. 12, 1975 retirement letter.

jj. During a Nov. 29, 1975, press conference, White House Press Secretary Ron Nessen revealed that the President had decided to nominate, as well as announce his choice of, Stevens the same day (Spencer Rich, "Ford Picks Chicago Jurist," *Washington Post*, Nov. 29, 1975, p. A1). The announcement occurred on Nov. 28, 1975.

kk. Although Justice Stewart's decision to retire was not made public until June 18, 1981, Stewart delivered a letter, stating his desire to retire, to President Ronald Reagan on May 18, 1981 (U.S. National Archives and Records Administration, Office of the Federal Register, *Public Papers of the Presidents of the United States: Ronald Reagan, 1981* (Washington: GPO, 1982), p. 539.

ll. In this case, the distinction between the dates of announcement of the nominee and the formal nomination is particularly important. On July 7, 1981, President Reagan "announced his intention" to nominate Judge O'Connor upon completion of a required FBI background check (U.S. National Archives and Records Administration, Office of the Federal Register, *Public Papers of the Presidents of the United States: Ronald Reagan, 1981,* (Washington: GPO, 1982), p. 597). President Reagan did not formally nominate her until Aug. 19, 1981, after she had passed the background check.

mm. Although Chief Justice Burger officially notified President Reagan, by letter on June 17, 1986, of his desire to retire, Burger privately informed Reagan of his plans on May 27, 1986 ("Remarks on the Resignation of Supreme Court Chief Justice Warren E. Burger and the Nominations of William H. Rehnquist To Be Chief Justice and Antonin Scalia To Be an Associate Justice," U.S. National Archives and Records Administration, Office of the Federal Register, *Public Papers of the Presidents of the United States: Ronald Reagan, 1986,* vol. 2 (Washington: GPO, 1989), p. 781).

nn. The May 27, 1986, date is used because Chief Justice Burger's intention to retire (known to President Reagan on May 27) alerted the President of the forthcoming opportunity to elevate Rehnquist from Associate Justice to Chief Justice, and in turn, of the opportunity to nominate someone to succeed Rehnquist as an Associate Justice.

oo. President Reagan reportedly "had no advance warning of the resignation" (Al Kamen, "Nixon-Appointed Democrat Cites Age, Health," *Washington Post*, June 27, 1987, p. A1).

pp. Judge Ginsburg withdrew his name from consideration before being officially nominated, but after President Reagan had announced his intention to nominate Ginsburg. Among other controversies surrounding the nomination, Ginsburg admitted shortly before withdrawing that he "had smoked marijuana while a Harvard law professor" (Lou Cannon and Ruth Markus, "Judge Kennedy Likely Choice," *Washington Post*, Nov. 9, 1987, p. A6).

qq. President George H. W. Bush stated in a July 23, 1990, press conference nominating Souter that he had not decided on a final nominee until that day (U.S. National Archives and Records Administration, Office of the Federal Register, *Public Papers of the Presidents of the United States: George Bush, 1990,* vol. 2 (Washington: GPO, 1992), p. 1051).

rr. On the details of transferring Justice White's retirement letter to the President beginning on Mar. 18, 1993, see Dennis J. Hutchinson, *The Man Who Was Once Whizzer White: A Portrait of Justice Byron R. White* (New York: Free Press , 1998, p. 437) and Ward, *Deciding to Leave,* p. 183, n. 183. One of Justice White's former law clerks, by then working in the White House, delivered the letter on the Mar. 19, 1993.

ss. President William J. Clinton announced Ginsburg's nomination on June 14, 1993. However, President Clinton noted in his nomination speech that he asked Ginsburg to accept the nomination on the evening of June 13 (U.S. National Archives and Records Administration, Office of the Federal Register, *Public Papers of the Presidents of the United States: William J. Clinton, 1993,* vol. 1 (Washington: GPO, 1994), p. 843).

tt. Jan. 1, 1994 is a slight estimation, since Justice Blackmun reportedly "told President Bill Clinton at Renaissance Weekend over the New Year's holiday in Hilton Head, S.C., that this would be his last term (Tony Mauro, "How Blackmun Hid Retirement Plans," *New Jersey Law Journal,* Apr. 25, 1994, p. 18.). Clinton publicly announced Blackmun's retirement on April 6, 1994. (U.S. National Archives and Records Administration, Office of the Federal Register, *Public Papers of the Presidents of the United States: William J. Clinton, 1994,* vol. 1 (Washington: GPO, 1995), p. 597).

Table 2. Duration in Days Between Major Events in the Supreme Court Nomination-and-Confirmation Process, 1900-2005

Nominating President	Outgoing Justice	Actual or Prospective Vacancy Apparently Became Known to President		Nominee	Number of days elapsed from . . .				
		When	How		Vacancy to nomination announcement	Nomination announcement to first hearing	First hearing to committee final action	Committee final action to Senate action	Starting date to final Senate action
Theodore Roosevelt	Horace Gray	09/15/1902	Death of outgoing Justice	Oliver Wendell Holmes	78	No record of hearing	No record of hearing	0	80
Theodore Roosevelt	George Shiras, Jr.	08/20/1902[a]	Public reports of imminent retirement	William R. Day	147	No record of hearing	No record of hearing	0	187
Theodore Roosevelt	Henry B. Brown	03/08/1906[b]	Outgoing Justice notified President of intention to retire[c]	William H. Moody	244	No record of hearing	No record of hearing	2	279

Table 2. (Continued)

Nominating President	Outgoing Justice	Actual or Prospective Vacancy Apparently Became Known to President		Nominee	Number of days elapsed from . . .				
		When	How		Vacancy to nomination announcement	Nomination announcement to first hearing	First hearing to committee final action	Committee final action to Senate action	Starting date to final Senate action
William Howard Taft	Rufus W. Peckham	10/24/1909	Death of outgoing Justice	Horace H. Lurton	50	No record of hearing	No record of hearing	4	59
William Howard Taft	David J. Brewer	03/28/1910	Death of outgoing Justice	Charles Evans Hughes	28	No record of hearing	No record of hearing	0	35
William Howard Taft	Melville W. Fuller *Chief Justice*	07/04/1910	Death of outgoing Chief Justice	Edward D. White	161	Nomination was not referred to Judiciary Committee	Nomination was not referred to Judiciary Committee	Nomination was not referred to Judiciary Committee	161

Table 2. (Continued)

Nominating President	Outgoing Justice	Actual or Prospective Vacancy Apparently Became Known to President		Nominee	Number of days elapsed from . . .				
		When	How		Vacancy to nomination announcement	Nomination announcement to first hearing	First hearing to committee final action	Committee final action to Senate action	Starting date to final Senate action
William Howard Taft	Edward D. White	12/12/1910	White nomination by President to be Chief Justice	Willis Van Devanter	0	No record of hearing	No record of hearing	0	3
William Howard Taft	William H. Moody	06/15/1910[d]	Congressional action authorizing retirement	Joseph R. Lamar	180	No record of hearing	No record of hearing	0	183
William Howard Taft	John Marshall Harlan	10/14/1911	Death of outgoing Justice	Mahlon Pitney	128	No record of hearing	No record of hearing	9	151

Table 2. (Continued)

Nominating President	Outgoing Justice	Actual or Prospective Vacancy Apparently Became Known to President		Nominee	Number of days elapsed from . . .				
		When	How		Vacancy to nomination announcement	Nomination announcement to first hearing	First hearing to committee final action	Committee final action to Senate action	Starting date to final Senate action
Woodrow Wilson	Horace H. Lurton	07/12/1914	Death of outgoing Justice	James C. McReynolds	38	No record of hearing	No record of hearing	5	48
Woodrow Wilson	Joseph R. Lamar	01/02/1916	Death of outgoing Justice	Louis D. Brandeis	26	12	105	8	151
Woodrow Wilson	Charles Evans Hughes	06/10/1916[e]	Resignation to pursue political office	John H. Clarke	34	No record of hearing	No record of hearing	0	44

Table 2. (Continued)

Nominating President	Outgoing Justice	Actual or Prospective Vacancy Apparently Became Known to President		Nominee	Number of days elapsed from . . .				
		When	How		Vacancy to nomination announcement	Nomination announcement to first hearing	First hearing to committee final action	Committee final action to Senate action	Starting date to final Senate action
Warren Harding	Edward D. White	05/19/1921	Death of outgoing Justice	William Howard Taft	42	Nomination was not referred to Judiciary Committee	Nomination was not referred to Judiciary Committee	Nomination was not referred to Judiciary Committee	42
Warren Harding	John H. Clarke	09/05/1922	Resignation letter submitted to President	George Sutherland	0	Nomination was not referred to Judiciary Committee	Nomination was not referred to Judiciary Committee	Nomination was not referred to Judiciary Committee	0

Table 2. (Continued)

Nominating President	Outgoing Justice	Actual or Prospective Vacancy Apparently Became Known to President		Nominee	Number of days elapsed from . . .				
		When	How		Vacancy to nomination announcement	Nomination announcement to first hearing	First hearing to committee final action	Committee final action to Senate action	Starting date to final Senate action
Warren Harding	William R. Day	09/05/1922[f]	Public reports of imminent retirement	Pierce Butler	79	No record of hearing	No record of hearing	No record of hearing	No final action
		12/04/1922	Lack of action on first nomination of Butler	Pierce Butler	1	No record of hearing	No record of hearing	3	4
Warren Harding	Mahlon Pitney	12/16/1922	White House announced forthcoming retirement[g]	Edward T. Sanford	24	No record of hearing	No record of hearing	0	44

Table 2. (Continued)

Nominating President	Outgoing Justice	Actual or Prospective Vacancy Apparently Became Known to President		Nominee	Number of days elapsed from . . .				
		When	How		Vacancy to nomination announcement	Nomination announcement to first hearing	First hearing to committee final action	Committee final action to Senate action	Starting date to final Senate action
Calvin Coolidge	Joseph McKenna	12/25/1924[h]	Public reports of imminent retirement	Harlan F. Stone	11	23	Committee vote to recommit before final action	0	32
							5	3	42
Herbert Hoover	William Howard Taft	02/03/1930	Retirement letter submitted to President	Charles Evans Hughes	0	No record of hearing	No record of hearing	3	10
Herbert Hoover	Edward T Sanford	03/08/1930	Death of outgoing Justice	John J. Parker	13	15	20	20	60

Table 2. (Continued)

Nominating President	Outgoing Justice	Actual or Prospective Vacancy Apparently Became Known to President		Nominee	Number of days elapsed from . . .				
		When	How		Vacancy to nomination announcement	Nomination announcement to first hearing	First hearing to committee final action	Committee final action to Senate action	Starting date to final Senate action
Herbert Hoover	Edward T. Sanford	05/07/1930	Parker nomination rejected by Senate	Owen J. Roberts	2	No record of hearing	No record of hearing	1	13
Herbert Hoover	Oliver Wendell Holmes, Jr.	01/12/1932	Outgoing Justice notified President of intention to retire	Benjamin N. Cardozo	34	No record of hearing	No record of hearing	1	43
Franklin D. Roosevelt	Willis Van Devanter	05/18/1937[i]	Retirement letter submitted to President	Hugo L. Black	86	No record of hearing	No record of hearing	1	91

Table 2. (Continued)

Nominating President	Outgoing Justice	Actual or Prospective Vacancy Apparently Became Known to President		Nominee	Number of days elapsed from . . .				
		When	How		Vacancy to nomination announcement	Nomination announcement to first hearing	First hearing to committee final action	Committee final action to Senate action	Starting date to final Senate action
Franklin D. Roosevelt	George Sutherland	01/05/1938	Retirement letter submitted to President	Stanley F. Reed	10	5	4	1	20
Franklin D. Roosevelt	Benjamin N. Cardozo	07/09/1938[j]	Death of outgoing Justice	Felix Frankfurter	180	2	9	1	192
Franklin D. Roosevelt	Louis D. Brandeis	02/13/1939[k]	Retirement letter submitted to President	William O. Douglas	35	4	3	8	50
Franklin D. Roosevelt	Pierce Butler	11/16/1939	Death of outgoing Justice	Frank Murphy	49	No record of hearing	No record of hearing	1	61

Table 2. (Continued)

Nominating President	Outgoing Justice	Actual or Prospective Vacancy Apparently Became Known to President		Nominee	Number of days elapsed from . . .				
		When	How		Vacancy to nomination announce-ment	Nomination announce-ment to first hearing	First hearing to committee final action	Committee final action to Senate action	Starting date to final Senate action
Franklin D. Roosevelt	James C. McReynolds	01/22/1941	Outgoing Justice notified President of intention to retire[l]	James F. Byrnes	141	Nomination was not referred to Judiciary Committee	Nomination was not referred to Judiciary Committee	Nomination was not referred to Judiciary Committee	141
Franklin D. Roosevelt	Charles Evans Hughes *Chief Justice*	06/02/1941[m]	Retirement letter submitted to President	Harlan F. Stone	10	9	2	4	25
Franklin D. Roosevelt	Harlan F. Stone	06/12/1941	Stone nomination by President to be Chief Justice	Robert H. Jackson	0	9	9	7	25

Table 2. (Continued)

Nominating President	Outgoing Justice	Actual or Prospective Vacancy Apparently Became Known to President		Nominee	Number of days elapsed from . . .				
		When	How		Vacancy to nomination announcement	Nomination announcement to first hearing	First hearing to committee final action	Committee final action to Senate action	Starting date to final Senate action
Franklin D. Roosevelt	James F. Byrnes	10/03/1942[n]	Byrnes appointment to other public office	Wiley B. Rutledge	100	11	10	7	128
Harry. S. Truman	Owen J. Roberts	06/30/1945[o]	Retirement letter submitted to President	Harold H. Burton	80	No record of hearing	No record of hearing	0	81
Harry S. Truman	Harlan F Stone *Chief Justice*	04/22/1946	Death of outgoing Chief Justice	Fred M. Vinson	45	8	5	1	59
Harry S. Truman	Frank Murphy	07/19/1949	Death of outgoing Justice	Thomas C. Clark	9	12	3	6	30

Table 2. (Continued)

Nominating President	Outgoing Justice	Actual or Prospective Vacancy Apparently Became Known to President		Nominee	Number of days elapsed from . . .				
		When	How		Vacancy to nomination announce-ment	Nomination announce-ment to first hearing	First hearing to committee final action	Committee final action to Senate action	Starting date to final Senate action
Harry S. Truman	Wiley B. Rutledge	09/10/1949	Death of outgoing Justice	Sherman Minton	5	12	6	1	24
Dwight D. Eisenhower	Fred M. Vinson *Chief Justice*	09/08/1953	Death of outgoing Chief Justice	Earl Warren	24	***Recess appointment, 10/02/1953***			
					125[P]	22	22	5	174
Dwight D. Eisenhower	Robert H. Jackson	10/09/1954	Death of outgoing Justice	John Marshall Harlan II	30	No record of hearing	No record committee action	No record of committee action	No record of final action after committee referral
					5	45	14	6	70

Table 2. (Continued)

Nominating President	Outgoing Justice	Actual or Prospective Vacancy Apparently Became Known to President		Nominee	Number of days elapsed from . . .				
		When	How		Vacancy to nomination announcement	Nomination announcement to first hearing	First hearing to committee final action	Committee final action to Senate action	Starting date to final Senate action
Dwight D. Eisenhower	Sherman Minton	09/07/1956	Retirement letter submitted to President	William J. Brennan	38	***Recess appointment, 10/15/1956***			
					129[q]	44	5	15	193
Dwight D. Eisenhower	Stanley F. Reed	01/31/1957	Press conference held by Reed announcing retirement[r]	Charles E. Whittaker	30	16	0	1	47
Dwight D. Eisenhower	Harold H. Burton	10/06/1958	Retirement letter submitted to President	Potter Stewart	8	***Recess appointment, 10/14/1958***			
					103[s]	82	11	15	211

Table 2. (Continued)

Nominating President	Outgoing Justice	Actual or Prospective Vacancy Apparently Became Known to President		Nominee	Number of days elapsed from . . .				
		When	How		Vacancy to nomination announce-ment	Nomination announce-ment to first hearing	First hearing to committee final action	Committee final action to Senate action	Starting date to final Senate action
John F. Kennedy	Charles E. Whittaker	03/28/1962	Retirement letter received by President[t]	Byron R. White	2	12	0	0	14
John F. Kennedy	Felix Frankfurter	08/28/1962[u]	Retirement letter submitted to President	Arthur J. Goldberg	1	13	14	0	28
Lyndon B. Johnson	Arthur J. Goldberg	07/20/1965	Goldberg appointment to other public office[v]	Abe Fortas	8	8	5	1	22

Table 2. (Continued)

Nominating President	Outgoing Justice	Actual or Prospective Vacancy Apparently Became Known to President		Nominee	Number of days elapsed from . . .				
		When	How		Vacancy to nomination announcement	Nomination announcement to first hearing	First hearing to committee final action	Committee final action to Senate action	Starting date to final Senate action
Lyndon B. Johnson	Thomas C. Clark	02/28/1967	Outgoing Justice notified President of intention to retire[w]	Thurgood Marshall	105	30	21	27	183
Lyndon B. Johnson	Earl Warren *Chief Justice*	06/13/1968[x]	Retirement letter submitted to President	Abe Fortas	13	15	77	5	110
Lyndon B. Johnson	Abe Fortas	06/26/1968[y]	Fortas nomination by Johnson to be Chief Justice	Homer Thornberry	0	15	No record of committee vote	No record of final committee action	100

Table 2. (Continued)

Nominating President	Outgoing Justice	Actual or Prospective Vacancy Apparently Became Known to President		Nominee	Number of days elapsed from . . .				
		When	How		Vacancy to nomination announcement	Nomination announcement to first hearing	First hearing to committee final action	Committee final action to Senate action	Starting date to final Senate action
Richard M. Nixon	Earl Warren *Chief Justice*	01/20/1969[z]	Fortas Chief Justice nomination withdrawn by President (10/4/1968)	Warren E. Burger	121	13	0	6	140

Table 2. (Continued)

Nominating President	Outgoing Justice	Actual or Prospective Vacancy Apparently Became Known to President		Nominee	Number of days elapsed from . . .				
		When	How		Vacancy to nomination announce-ment	Nomination announce-ment to first hearing	First hearing to committee final action	Committee final action to Senate action	Starting date to final Senate action
Richard M. Nixon	Abe Fortas	05/14/1969	Resignation letter submitted to President	Clement F. Haynsworth, Jr.	96	29	23	43	191
		11/21/1969	Haynsworth nomination rejected by Senate	G. Harrold Carswell	59	8	20	51	138
		04/08/1970	Carswell nomination rejected by Senate	Harry A. Blackmun	8	15	7	6	34

Table 2. (Continued)

Nominating President	Outgoing Justice	Actual or Prospective Vacancy Apparently Became Known to President		Nominee	Number of days elapsed from . . .				
		When	How		Vacancy to nomination announcement	Nomination announcement to first hearing	First hearing to committee final action	Committee final action to Senate action	Starting date to final Senate action
Richard M. Nixon	Hugo L. Black	09/17/1971	Retirement letter submitted to President	Lewis F. Powell, Jr.	34	13	20	13	80
Richard M. Nixon	John Marshall Harlan II	09/23/1971	Retirement letter submitted to President	William H. Rehnquist	28	13	20	17	78
Gerald R. Ford	William O. Douglas	11/12/1975 [aa]	Retirement letter submitted to President	John Paul Stevens	16	10	3	6	35

Table 2. (Continued)

Nominating President	Outgoing Justice	Actual or Prospective Vacancy Apparently Became Known to President		Nominee	Number of days elapsed from . . .				
		When	How		Vacancy to nomination announcement	Nomination announcement to first hearing	First hearing to committee final action	Committee final action to Senate action	Starting date to final Senate action
Ronald Reagan	Potter Stewart	05/18/1981 [bb]	Retirement letter submitted to President	Sandra Day O'Connor	50	64	6	6	126
Ronald Reagan	Warren E. Burger *Chief Justice*	05/27/1986 [cc]	Justice privately alerted President of intention to retire	William H. Rehnquist	21	42	16	34	113
Ronald Reagan	William H. Rehnquist	05/27/1986 [dd]	Rehnquist nomination by Reagan to be Chief Justice	Antonin Scalia	21	49	9	34	113

Table 2. (Continued)

Nominating President	Outgoing Justice	Actual or Prospective Vacancy Apparently Became Known to President		Nominee	Number of days elapsed from . . .				
		When	How		Vacancy to nomination announce-ment	Nomination announce-ment to first hearing	First hearing to committee final action	Committee final action to Senate action	Starting date to final Senate action
Ronald Reagan	Lewis F. Powell, Jr.	06/26/1987 [ee]	Press conference held by Powell announcing retirement	Robert H. Bork	5	76	21	17	119
		10/23/1987	Bork nomination rejected by Senate	Douglas H. Ginsburg	6	Ginsburg withdrew (11/07/1987) before official nomination[ff]			
		11/07/1987	Ginsburg withdrawal	Anthony M. Kennedy	4	33	44	7	88

Table 2. (Continued)

Nominating President	Outgoing Justice	Actual or Prospective Vacancy Apparently Became Known to President		Nominee	Number of days elapsed from . . .				
		When	How		Vacancy to nomination announcement	Nomination announcement to first hearing	First hearing to committee final action	Committee final action to Senate action	Starting date to final Senate action
George H. W. Bush	William J. Brennan	07/20/1990	Retirement letter submitted to President	David H. Souter	3	52	14	5	74
George H. W. Bush	Thurgood Marshall	06/27/1991	Retirement letter submitted to President	Clarence Thomas	4	71	17	18	110
William J. Clinton	Byron R. White	03/19/1993 [gg]	Retirement letter submitted to President	Ruth Bader Ginsburg	87	36	9	5	137

Table 2. (Continued)

Nominating President	Outgoing Justice	Actual or Prospective Vacancy Apparently Became Known to President		Nominee	Number of days elapsed from . . .				
		When	How		Vacancy to nomination announcement	Nomination announcement to first hearing	First hearing to committee final action	Committee final action to Senate action	Starting date to final Senate action
William J. Clinton	Harry A. Blackmun	01/01/1994 [hh]	Justice privately alerted President	Stephen G. Breyer	132	60	7	10	209

Table 2. (Continued)

Nominating President	Outgoing Justice	Actual or Prospective Vacancy Apparently Became Known to President		Nominee	Number of days elapsed from . . .				
		When	How		Vacancy to nomination announcement	Nomination announcement to first hearing	First hearing to committee final action	Committee final action to Senate action	Starting date to final Senate action
George W. Bush	Sandra Day O'Connor	07/01/2005	Retirement letter submitted to President	John G. Roberts	18	Nomination withdrawn by President (09/05/2005), re-nominated as Chief Justice (09/05/2005)	No opportunity for final Senate action	No opportunity for final Senate action	No opportunity for final Senate action
		09/05/2005	Announcement of Roberts nomination withdrawal and re-submission by President	Harriet Miers	30				

Table 2. (Continued)

Nominating President	Outgoing Justice	Actual or Prospective Vacancy Apparently Became Known to President		Nominee	Number of days elapsed from . . .				
		When	How		Vacancy to nomination announcement	Nomination announcement to first hearing	First hearing to committee final action	Committee final action to Senate action	Starting date to final Senate action
George W. Bush	William H. Rehnquist	09/03/2005	Death of outgoing Justice	John G. Roberts	2	7	10	7	26

Sources: Durations for major intervals in the nomination-and-confirmation process were computed by the CRS authors. As described in the text, this research relied on historical newspapers, official presidential papers, and CRS correspondence with Presidential Libraries. Ward's *Deciding to Leave* was especially useful in compiling data on the reasons why Justices left the bench. Additional source information appears in the table notes below.

a. It is unclear when President Theodore Roosevelt learned of Justice Shiras's intention to retire. However, *Washington Post* coverage suggests that Shiras's forthcoming departure was well known in Washington by at least Aug. 20, 1902 ("Knox May Not Want It: Belief that He Would Decline Justice Shiras' Position," *Washington Post*, Aug. 20, 1902, p. 1).

b. According to the *Washington Post*, Justice Brown notified the President, on Mar. 8, 1906, that he wished to retire ("To Leave the Bench: Justice Brown Will Retire in the Fall," *Washington Post*, Mar. 8, 1906, p. 3).

c. It is unclear from the historical record whether the President learned of Justice Brown's desire to retire by letter, personal conversation, etc.

d. Justice Moody did not actually depart the Court until Nov. 20, 1910 (Ward, *Deciding to Leave*, p. 5). However, "Illness of a serious nature has kept Justice Moody from his duties in the Supreme Court for almost a year. There have been occasional rumors of retirement, but Senator Lodge [on June 15, 1910] presented the real harbinger of that action, in the form of a bill extending the statute relating to retirement from the Supreme Court to cover the case of Mr. Moody" ("Moody Will Retire," *Washington Post*, June 15, 1910, p. 1).

e. On June 10, 1916, Justice Hughes resigned to pursue the 1916 Republican presidential nomination ("Hughes, With Words That Ring, Obeys Call to Lead Republicans," *Washington Post*, June 11, 1916, p. 1). Although historical media research does not indicate that President Wilson knew for certain that Justice Hughes would resign, media reports had hinted at a Hughes resignation throughout the spring of 1916.

f. Day did not leave the Court until Nov. 13, 1922. However, the *Washington Post* reported that Day's consideration of retirement was mentioned at a White House briefing on Sept. 5, 1922 ("Justice Day May Leave the Bench," *Washington Post*, Sept. 6, 1922, p. 1).

g. Although Justice Pitney's resignation was effective as of Dec. 31, 1922, the White House announced Pitney's forthcoming departure on Dec. 16, 1922 ("Resigns," *Chicago Daily Tribune*, Dec. 17, 1922, p. 17).

h. Justice McKenna did not officially retire until Jan. 5, 1925. However, the media reported his imminent retirement on Dec. 25, 1924 ("M'Kenna to Retire Soon as a Justice of the Supreme Court," *Washington Post*, Dec. 25, 1924, p. 2).

i. For an account of Justice Van Devanter privately alerting a reporter of his decision to retire on the morning of the announcement, see "News 'Beat' Aided by Van Devanter," *New York Times*, May 23, 1937, p. 40.

j. Although Justice Cardozo had been ill and away from the bench since December 1937 (United Press, "Supreme Court Liberal Succumbs to Heart Ailment in N.Y.," *Washington Post*, July 10, 1938, p. M1), a definite need to nominate a new Justice did not occur until Cardozo's death on July 9, 1938.

k. Justice Brandeis had been away from the bench for a month, recovering from a heart attack, prior to announcing his retirement (United Press, "Justice Brandeis, Dean of Supreme Court, Quits," *Los Angeles Times*, Feb. 14, 1939, p. 1). Nonetheless, his retirement was considered abrupt, suggesting that President Roosevelt had little advance notice to consider a successor.

l. It is unclear from the historical record whether the President learned of Justice McReynolds's desire to retire by letter, personal conversation, etc.

m. Although Chief Justice Hughes's retirement due to age and poor health had been "rumored some months" prior to submission of his formal retirement letter (Walter Trohan, "Hughes Retires From Court," *Chicago Daily Tribune*, June 3, 1941, p. 1), the definite need for a new nominee did not arise until Hughes announced his retirement.

n. Justice Byrnes resigned at President Roosevelt's request on Oct. 3, 1942, becoming Director of Economic Stability. Roosevelt was, therefore, aware of an impending vacancy on the Court prior to the formal resignation, although the precise date is unclear. For a summary of Byrnes's transition from the Court to his new post, see Associated Press, "Byrnes Resigns From Bench in Letter to President," *New York Times*, Oct. 4, 1942, p. 45.

o. Although President Truman did not announce Justice Roberts's intention to retire until July 5, 1945 (United Press, "Morganthau and Roberts Resign," *Los Angeles Times*, July 6, 1945, p. 1), Justice Roberts's retirement letter is dated June 30, 1945. Truman received the letter on that date "or soon thereafter" (e-mail communication between CRS Information Specialist Dana Ely and Truman Library Archivist Randy Sowell, Sept. 2, 2005).

p. Congress was not in session when Chief Justice Vinson died on Sept. 8, 1953 (U.S. Congress, Joint Committee on Printing, *2003-2004 Official Congressional Directory: 108th Congress* (Washington: GPO), p. 519). President Eisenhower recess-appointed Earl Warren as Chief Justice on Oct. 2, 1953 and nominated him to the Court, on Jan. 11, 1954, after Congress reconvened for the second session of the 83rd Congress. Therefore, although the interval between the starting date (Sept. 8, 1953, as shown in Table 1) and announcement date (Jan. 11, 1954) is 125 days, and the entire interval from the starting date until final Senate action (Mar. 1, 1954) is 174 days, the President's actual decisionmaking timetable could also be classified as 24 days, or the interval between Vinson's death (Sept. 8, 1953) and Eisenhower's recess appointment of Chief Justice Warren (Oct. 2, 1953). Both intervals are used to calculate the median elapsed time from vacancy to nomination announcement. Nonetheless, the long intervals have a minimal impact on computing the median durations between stages in the process because the median is less sensitive than the mean to extremely high or low values.

q. Congress was not in session when Justice Minton submitted his retirement letter to the President on Sept. 7, 1956 (U.S. Congress, Joint Committee on Printing, *2003-2004 Official Congressional Directory: 108th Congress*,\ (Washington: GPO), p. 519). President Eisenhower recess-appointed William J. Brennan as Associate Justice on Oct. 15, 1956, and nominated him to the Court, on Jan. 14, 1957, after Congress convened for the first session of the 85th Congress. Therefore, although the interval between the starting date (Sept. 7, 1956, as shown in Table 1) and announcement date (Jan. 14, 1957) is 129 days, and the entire interval from the starting date until final Senate action (Mar. 19, 1957) is 193 days, the President's actual decision-making timetable could also be classified as 38 days, or the interval between Brennan's retirement announcement (Sept. 7, 1956) and Eisenhower's recess appointment of Justice Brennan (Oct. 15, 1956). Both intervals are used to calculate the median elapsed time from vacancy to nomination announcement. Nonetheless, the long intervals have a minimal impact on computing the median durations between stages in the process because median is less sensitive than the mean to extremely high or low values.

r. Whether President Eisenhower first learned of Justice Reed's retirement through the press conference or a letter from Reed is unclear. Contemporary media coverage mentioned a press conference and a letter to Eisenhower (Edward T. Folliard, "Reed Is Retiring From High Court," *Washington Post*, Feb. 1, 1957, p. A1). However, political scientist Artemus Ward's account asserts that Reed announced his retirement through a press conference (Ward, *Deciding to Leave*, pp. 162-163). Regardless, both events occurred on Jan. 31, 1957. For the Jan. 31 correspondence between Reed and Eisenhower, see "Letter to Stanley Reed Regarding His Retirement From Active Service as An Associate Justice of the Supreme Court," U.S. National Archives and Records Administration, Office of the Federal Register, *Public Papers of the Presidents of the United States: Dwight D. Eisenhower, 1957* (Washington: GPO, 1958), pp. 109-110.

s. Congress was not in session when Burton submitted his retirement letter to the President on Oct. 6, 1958 (U.S. Congress, Joint Committee on Printing,*2003-2004 Official Congressional Directory: 108th Congress* (Washington: GPO), p. 519). President Eisenhower recess-appointed Potter Stewart as Associate Justice on Oct. 14, 1958, and nominated him to the Court, on Jan. 17, 1959, after Congress convened for the first session of the 86th Congress. Therefore, although the interval between the starting date (Oct. 6, 1958, as shown in Table 1) and nomination date (Jan. 17, 1959) is 103 days, and the entire interval from the starting date until final Senate action (May 5, 1959) is 211 days, the President's actual decision-making timetable could also be classified as 8 days, or the interval between Burton's retirement announcement (Oct. 6, 1958) and Eisenhower's recess appointment of Justice Stewart (Oct. 14, 1958). Both intervals are used to calculate the median elapsed time from vacancy to nomination announcement. Nonetheless, the long intervals have a minimal impact on computing the median durations between stages in the process because the median is less sensitive than the mean to extremely high or low values.

t. This information is based on e-mail communication between CRS Information Specialist Dana Ely and Kennedy Library Reference Technician Sharon Kelly, Sept. 14, 2005.

u. Aug. 28, 1962, is the only definitive date which can be established based on available data, as the earliest point at which President Kennedy learned of Justice Frankfurter's intention to retire. However, President Kennedy's quick nomination of Goldberg, and Justice Frankfurter's poor health in the weeks leading up to his retirement, suggest that President Kennedy was considering prospective nominees well before Frankfurter stepped down. Kennedy's letter to Justice Frankfurter accepting his retirement references a visit the President paid to Frankfurter to check on his health sometime during the summer of 1962 (U.S. National Archives and Records Administration, Office of the Federal Register, *Public Papers of the Presidents of the United States: John F. Kennedy, 1962*, (Washington: GPO, 1963), p. 656). According to Kennedy Library Reference Technician Sharon Kelly, Kennedy's office files suggest that correspondence between Frankfurter, Special Assistant for National Security Affairs McGeorge Bundy, and the President would have alerted Kennedy to Frankfurter's declining health around May 17, 1962 (e-mail communication between CRS Information Specialist Dana Ely and Kennedy Library Reference Technician Sharon Kelly, Sept. 14, 2005).

v. President Lyndon B. Johnson unexpectedly nominated Justice Goldberg to be U.S. Ambassador to the United Nations following the death on July 14, 1965, of the previous ambassador, Adlai E. Stevenson. See Carroll Kilpatrick, "Goldberg is Named to Stevenson Post," *Washington Post*, July 21, 1965, p. A1.

w. Despite the fact that Justice Clark announced his forthcoming retirement on Feb. 28, 1967, historical evidence suggests that Johnson might have prompted Clark's retirement as early as Jan. 1967, when the President prepared to nominated Justice Clark's son, Ramsey, to be Attorney General. "On January 25, 1967, Johnson told Ramsey that he could only be named the permanent attorney general if his father stepped down from the Court" (Ward, *Deciding to Leave*, p. 170).

x. Although President Johnson did not announce Chief Justice Warren's retirement until June 26, he received Warren's retirement letter on June 13, 1968 (U.S. National Archives and Records Administration, Office of the Federal Register, *Public Papers of the Presidents of the United States: Lyndon B. Johnson, 1968-69*, vol. 1 (Washington: GPO, 1966), p. 746).

y. Although a specific opportunity to name a new Associate Justice did not arise until the Fortas Chief Justice nomination on June 26, 1968, it was reported that "[s]ome Texans at the Capitol are sure that Mr. Johnson has planned for the last four years to name Thornberry to the Supreme Court before he [Johnson] left office," (Richard L. Lyons, "Homer Thornberry: 'Constructive Liberal,' Close LBJ friend," *Washington Post,* June 27, 1969, p. 1).

z. Jan. 20, 1969 (the date of Richard M. Nixon's inauguration), is used as the starting date for the vacancy because it marks the beginning of President Nixon's official decision-making powers. After the Abe Fortas Chief Justice nomination failed, President Johnson announced on Oct. 2, 1968, that he would not name another nominee (U.S. National Archives and Records Administration, Office of the Federal Register, *Public Papers of the Presidents of the United States: Lyndon B. Johnson, 1968-69*, vol. 2 (Washington: GPO, 1966), p. 509). Eight days later, Johnson elaborated on his decision. The President wrote that although he would have made another nomination in "ordinary times," the situation was extraordinary and that, "Under the circumstances, the foundations of government would be better served by the present Chief Justice [Earl Warren] remaining [in office] until emotionalism subsides, reason and fairness prevail (U.S. National Archives and Records Administration, Office of the Federal Register, *Public Papers of the Presidents of the United States: Lyndon B. Johnson, 1968-69*, vol. 2 (Washington: GPO, 1970), p. 1024). On Dec. 3, 1968, Chief Justice Warren informed President-elect Richard M. Nixon that he was willing to continue serving until a successor was confirmed ("Statement by the Chief Justice," Dec. 4, 1968, Earl Warren Papers, Manuscript Division, Library of Congress, Washington, DC). In a May 1969, conversation with reporters, President Nixon offered an unusually detailed discussion of his decision-making process surrounding the Burger nomination. Nixon reported that he thought "it would not be a proper mark of respect for the Court and for the Chief Justice to have a nomination go down, say, in February or March, and then have possibly the Senate hearings and the like at a time that the Court was sitting," and that his target date for a nomination decision was between May 1 and June 1, 1968 (U.S. National Archives and Records Administration, Office of the Federal Register, *Public Papers of the Presidents of the United States: Richard Nixon, 1970*, (Washington: GPO, 1971), p. 390).

aa Chief Justice Warren Burger reportedly "hint[ed] at a possible vacancy" on the Court in a letter to President Gerald Ford on Nov. 10, 1975, and offered "factors for [the President] to consider when appointing a new justice" (e-mail communication between CRS Information Specialist Dana Ely and Ford Library Archivist Technician Joshua Cochran, Sept. 12, 2005). Justice Douglas's health had been in question since Dec. 31, 1974, when he suffered a stroke (John P. MacKenzie, "Douglas Retires From Court," *Washington Post*, Nov. 13, 1975, p. A1). However, President Ford would have had relatively little time to consider a replacement Justice since he did not assume the presidency until Aug. 9, 1975, and a vacancy did not officially arise until Justice Douglas's Nov. 12, 1975 retirement letter.

bb. Although Justice Stewart's decision to retire was not made public until June 18, 1981, Stewart delivered a letter, stating his desire to retire, to President Ronald Reagan on May 18, 1981 (U.S. National Archives and Records Administration, Office of the Federal Register, *Public Papers of the Presidents of the United States: Ronald Reagan, 1981* (Washington: GPO, 1982), p. 539).

cc. Although Chief Justice Burger officially notified President Reagan of his desire to retire, by letter on June 17, 1986, Burger privately informed Reagan of his plans on May 27, 1986 ("Remarks on the Resignation of Supreme Court Chief Justice Warren E. Burger and the Nominations of William H. Rehnquist To Be Chief Justice and Antonin Scalia To Be an Associate Justice," U.S. National Archives and Records Administration, Office of the Federal Register, *Public Papers of the Presidents of the United States: Ronald Reagan, 1986,* vol. 2 (Washington: GPO, 1989), p. 781).

dd. The May 27, 1986, date is used because Chief Justice Burger's intention to retire (known to President Reagan on May 27) alerted the President of the forthcoming opportunity to elevate Rehnquist from Associate Justice to Chief Justice, and in turn, of the opportunity to nominate someone to succeed Rehnquist as an Associate Justice.

ee. President Reagan reportedly "had no advance warning of the resignation" (Al Kamen, "Nixon-Appointed Democrat Cites Age, Health," *Washington Post*, June 27, 1987, p. A1).

ff. Judge Ginsburg withdrew his name from consideration before being officially nominated, but after President Reagan had announced his intention to nominate Ginsburg. Among other controversies surrounding the nomination, Ginsburg admitted shortly before withdrawing that he "had smoked marijuana while a Harvard law professor" (Lou Cannon and Ruth Markus, "Judge Kennedy Likely Choice," *Washington Post*, Nov. 9, 1987, p. A6).

gg. On the details of transferring Justice White's retirement letter to the President beginning on Mar. 18, 1993, see Dennis J. Hutchinson, *The Man Who Was Once Whizzer White: A Portrait of Justice Byron R. White* (New York: Free Press , 1998, p. 437) and Ward, *Deciding to Leave,* p. 183, n. 183. One of Justice White's former law clerks, by then working in the White House, delivered the letter on the Mar. 19, 1993.

hh. Jan. 1, 1994, is an estimation, since Justice Blackmun reportedly "told President Bill Clinton at Renaissance Weekend over the New Year's holiday in Hilton Head, S.C., that this would be his last term (Tony Mauro, "How Blackmun Hid Retirement Plans," *New Jersey Law Journal,* Apr. 25, 1994, p. 18.). Clinton publicly announced Blackmun's retirement on April 6, 1994. (U.S. National Archives and Records Administration, Office of the Federal Register, *Public Papers of the Presidents of the United States: William J. Clinton, 1994,* vol. 1 (Washington: GPO), 1995, p. 597).

Table 3. Median Duration in Days Between Major Events in the Supreme Court Nomination-and-Confirmation Process, 1900-2005

Time Period	Median Number of Days Elapsed From . . .[a]					
	President Apparently Learned of Actual or Prospective Vacancy to Nomination Announcement	Nomination Announcement to First Hearing	First Hearing to Committee Final Action	Committee Final Action to Senate Action	Nomination Announcement to Final Senate Action	President Apparently Learned of Actual or Prospective Vacancy to Final Senate Action
1900-1980	34	13	9	3	28[c]	59
1981-2005	18	51	12	9[b]	84[d]	113
1900-2005	29	15	9	5	50	74

Sources: Durations for major intervals in the nomination-and-confirmation process were computed by the CRS authors. As described in the text, this research relied on historical newspapers, official presidential papers, and CRS correspondence with Presidential Libraries. Ward's *Deciding to Leave* was especially useful in compiling data on the reasons why Justices left the bench.

a. In Table 3, the median amount of time from vacancy to final Senate action within each time period does not necessarily equal the sum of the medians for each stage in the nominationand-confirmation process. Likewise, the median length of time for all Senate actions (i.e., from nomination announcement to final Senate action) within each time period does not equal the sum of the medians for each stage. The median identifies the mid-point for individual sets of observations. Because each stage of the process can have a different number of observations, and because the data are also not a "normal" (i.e., "bell-shaped") distribution, the sum of the medians for individual stages generally is not equal to the median for the entire period. For more information, see chapter 4 in Ya-lun Chou, *Statistical Analysis for Business and Economics* (New York: Elsevier, 1989).

b. The actual median is 8.5 days, which is rounded to 9 days for the purposes of this report.

c. The actual median is 27.5, which is rounded to 28 days for the purposes of this report.

d. The medians for the interval (duration) between the nomination announcement and final Senate action from 1981-2005 and 1900-2005, listed in Table 3 do not include John G. Roberts's Chief Justice confirmation because of the unusual circumstances surrounding the withdrawal of Roberts's nomination for Associate Justice, and his re-nomination for Chief Justice. The median duration for Senate action when *including* the John G. Roberts Chief Justice confirmation is 81 days (rounded from 80.5) from 1981-2005 and 50 days from 1900-2005.

Note: For a listing of all Supreme Court nominations made during the 1900-2005 period and, for each nomination, the dates of the "major events" accounted for in the columns in Table 3, see the preceding Table 1. For a listing, for each nomination, of the duration in da

REFERENCES

[1] CRS Information Specialist Maureen Bearden lent substantial research expertise to this report, former CRS intern Alvin Huynh provided initial research assistance, and CRS Specialist in American National Government Curtis Copeland provided helpful input. In addition, CRS Senior Production Assistants Mildred Boyle and JoAnn Thomas provided formatting assistance.

[2] Justice O'Connor's retirement letter is available at: [http://www.supreme courtus.gov/publicinfo/press/oconnor070105.pdf].

[3] "Senate GOP Leaders Seek Quick Action on Nominee to Replace Justice O'Connor," *Daily Report for Executives*, July 5, 2005, p. A-33.

[4] See [http://www.whitehouse.gov/news/releases/2005/10/20051003.html] for a copy of the President's nomination statement and Miers's remarks.

[5] 5 See [http://www.whitehouse.gov/news/releases/2005/10/20051004-1.html] for the text of this press conference.

[6] See [http://frist.senate.gov/index.cfm?FuseAction=Speeches.DetailandSpeech_id=293] for a copy of Senator Frist's statement.

[7] Kimberly Heffling, "Specter Decries Bush 'Pummeling' on Miers," *Washington Post*, Oct. 11, 2005 [http://www.washingtonpost.com/wp-dyn/content/article/2005/10/11/AR2005101101310.html].

[8] John Stanton, "Leaders Seeking To Place Miers On Court By Thanksgiving," *CongressDailyPM*, Oct. 3, 2005.

[9] Sheryl Gay Stolberg, "Some Liberals and Conservatives Find Themselves in Awkward Spots," *New York Times*, Oct. 4, 2005, p. A23.

[10] U.S. National Archives and Records Administration, Office of the Federal Register, *Public Papers of the Presidents of the United States: William J. Clinton, 1993,* vol. 1 (Washington: GPO, 1994), p. 597.

[11] U.S. National Archives and Records Administration, Office of the Federal Register, *Public Papers of the Presidents of the United States: Ronald Reagan, 1981* (Washington: GPO, 1982), p. 596.

[12] U. S. Congress, Senate, *Journal of the Executive Proceedings of the Senate of the United States of America*, 97th Cong., 1st sess., Aug. 19, 1981 (Washington: GPO, 1982), p. 644.

[13] Although these three events usually occur on the same day, a nomination sometimes, on rare occasions, is received by the Senate on a day after it was signed by the President, or is referred to the Judiciary Committee on a day after its receipt by the Senate.

[14] For an analysis of all unsuccessful Supreme Court nominees up to 2004, see CRS Report RL31171, *Supreme Court Nominations Not Confirmed, 1789-2004*, by Henry B. Hogue. In addition to the unsuccessful nominations listed in that report for the 1900-2004 period, the present report includes Judge Douglas H. Ginsburg as a an unsuccessful "nominee" since one part of the report's focus is on presidential announcements of nominees. President Reagan announced his *intention* to nominate Judge Ginsburg in 1987, but Ginsburg withdrew his name from consideration before being officially nominated. The Ginsburg case is briefly discussed later in this report.

[15] This particularly is the case for coverage of Supreme Court appointments in on-line fulltext historical newspapers, where coverage, as might be expected, typically is found to be less comprehensive regarding the procedures of Supreme Court appointments farther back into the 19th century.

[16] The earliest Supreme Court confirmation hearings held in open session were those in 1916 for the nomination of Louis D. Brandeis to be an Associate Justice. See CRS Report RL31989, *Supreme Court Appointment Process: Roles of the President, Judiciary Committee, and Senate*, by Denis Steven Rutkus, p. 19.

[17] Consulting National Archives and Records Administration (NARA) presidential libraries and records projects to investigate diaries and other records for evidence of private correspondence between Presidents and outgoing Justices is an ongoing project. CRS Knowledge Services Group Information Research Specialist Dana Ely, Karen Anson (Franklin D. Roosevelt Library), Valoise Armstrong (Eisenhower Library), Joshua Cochran (Ford Library), Jennifer Evans (Nixon Presidential Materials), Sharon Kelly (Kennedy Library), Matthew Schaefer (Hoover Library), Randy Sowell (Truman Library), Jennifer Sternaman (Reagan Library), Deborah Wheeler (George Bush Library), and Adam C. Bergfeld (Clinton Library) provided assistance on this portion of the project.

[18] U.S. Constitution, Article III, Sec. 1.

[19] Under 28 U.S.C. §371, Supreme Court Justices, like other Article III (tenure "during good Behaviour") federal judges, may *retire*, and be entitled to receive retirement compensation, in one of two ways — either by taking "senior status" or by "retiring from office." Beginning at age 65, they are entitled to receive retirement compensation, if having served a minimum 10 years as an Article III judge, their age and overall Article III judicial experience totals 80 years. (Hence, under this "Rule of 80," a Justice of age

65 must have served 15 years to become eligible for retirement compensation; a Justice of age 66, 14 years; a Justice of age 67, 13 years; etc.) Judges who take senior status retire from regular active service but retain their judicial office and the salary of the office, subject to annual certification of their having performed certain judicial or administrative duties in the preceding year. Judges who retire from office completely relinquish their judicial office with the right to a frozen lifetime annuity equal to the salary of the office at the time of retirement. In contrast, a Justice's *resignation* entails voluntarily relinquishing his or her judicial office without meeting the age and service requirements of the Rule of 80 (and thus being ineligible to receive retirement compensation). See U.S. Administrative Office of the United States Courts, *Senior Status and Retirement for Article III Judges*, Apr. 1999 (Judges Information Series, No. 4), pp. vii-viii.

[20] Carroll Kilpatrick, "Goldberg is Named to Stevenson Post," *Washington Post*, July 21, 1965, p. A1.

[21] On the controversies surrounding Justice Fortas's nomination and resignation, see Artemus Ward, *Deciding to Leave: The Politics of Retirement from the United States Supreme Court* (Albany: State University of New York Press, 2003), pp. 171-175; and Philip Warden and Aldo Beckman, "Fortas Agrees to Quit, Nixon Aide Says," *Chicago Tribune*, May 15, 1969, p. 7.

[22] The law provides that a Justice retiring under these provisions shall receive for the remainder of his lifetime "the salary he is receiving at the date of retirement" or, if his service were less than ten years, one-half of that salary. Act of August 5, 1939, ch. 433, 53 Stat. 1204-1205; 28 U.S.C. §372(a).

[23] "Moody Will Retire," *Washington Post*, June 15, 1910, p. 1.

[24] The other Associate Justices nominated for Chief Justice during the period were: Edward D. White (1910), Harlan F. Stone (1941), and Abe Fortas (1968). As noted previously, Justice Fortas's nomination failed to receive Senate confirmation.

[25] "Hughes, With Words That Ring, Obeys Call to Lead Republicans," *Washington Post*, Junc 11, 1916, p. 1.

[26] Associated Press, "Byrnes Resigns From Bench in Letter to President," *New York Times*, Oct. 4, 1942, p. 45.

[27] On the controversies surrounding Justice Fortas's nomination and resignation, see Ward, *Deciding to Leave*, pp. 171-175; and Philip Warden and Aldo Beckman, "Fortas Agrees to Quit, Nixon Aide Says," *Chicago Tribune*, May 15, 1969, p. 7.

[28] Haynsworth and Carswell were both rejected due to Senate doubts about their personal views and professional qualifications. For a summary of these and other cases of rejected Supreme Court nominees, see Hogue, *Supreme Court Nominations Not Confirmed, 1789-2004*.

[29] In Table 3, the median amount of time from vacancy to final Senate action within each time period does not necessarily equal the sum of the medians for each stage in the nomination-and-confirmation process. Likewise, the median length of time for all Senate actions (i.e., from nomination announcement to final Senate action) within each time period do not equal the sum of the medians for each stage. The median identifies the mid-point for individual sets of observations. Because each stage of the process can have a different number of observations, and because the data are also not a "normal" (i.e., "bell-shaped") distribution, the sum of the medians for individual stages generally is not equal to the median for the entire period. For more information, see chapter 4 in Ya-lun Chou, *Statistical Analysis for Business and Economics* (New York: Elsevier, 1989).

[30] In Tables 1 and 2, actual vacancies are those that already have been announced or occurred (i.e., a sitting Justice announces a retirement date or dies). Prospective vacancies, for the purposes of this report, are not merely speculative. They require firm notice, either through notification from a sitting Justice or major media accounts, that a Justice will leave the Court imminently, even if an exact date is not specified.

[31] This report, it should be re-emphasized, bases the starting point at when Presidents apparently learned of actual or prospective Court vacancies. These dates are based on published information or information obtained from presidential archives. Readers should be alerted, as a caveat, that there might well have been instances, unreported at the time as well as still unknown to present-day scholars, in which various Presidents privately were alerted of upcoming Court vacancies or had reasons to believe that vacancies were imminent in advance of the starting dates listed in this report. To the extent that such instances are unaccounted for, the full extent of time during which such Presidents were aware of prospective Court vacancies and were able to consider future Court candidates before publicly announcing their choices, is under-measured in this report.

[32] As noted elsewhere in this report, President George W. Bush withdrew Roberts's nomination as Associate Justice on Sept. 5, 2005.

[33] President Reagan had a private conversation with Chief Justice Burger on May 27, 1986, when Burger alerted the President to his impending retirement ("Remarks on the Resignation of Supreme Court Chief Justice

Warren E. Burger and the Nominations of William H. Rehnquist To Be Chief Justice and Antonin Scalia To Be an Associate Justice," U.S. National Archives and Records Administration, Office of the Federal Register, *Public Papers of the Presidents of the United States: Ronald Reagan, 1986,* vol. 2 (Washington: GPO, 1989) p. 781).

[34] President Truman did not announce that Clark had accepted the nomination until Aug. 1, 1949 (Edward T. Folliard, "Clark Accepts High Court Proffer," *Washington Post*, Aug. 2, 1949), p. 1.

[35] When calculating durations, the date on which the final event occurs is not counted as a full day. For example, if committee hearings began on July 12 and the committee took its final action on July 13, the duration is one day, not two. For cases in which durations are less than one day (i.e., the committee final action and final Senate vote took place on the same day), the duration is listed as 0 days.

[36] Although the arithmetic mean (the sum of all observations divided by the number of observations) is the true "average" number, it has the disadvantage of being skewed by extremely high or low values. For an introduction to median versus mean and arguments surrounding when each should be used, see chapter 3 in Alan Agresti and Barbara Finlay, *Statistical Methods for the Social Sciences*, 3rd ed. (Upper Saddle River, NJ: Prentice Hall, 1997).

[37] William H. Greene, *Econometric Analysis*, 5th ed. (Upper Saddle River, NJ: Prentice Hall, 2003, p. 847).

[38] As previously noted, although Chief Justice Burger, by letter on June 17, 1986, officially notified President Reagan of his desire to retire, Burger privately informed Reagan of his plans on May 27, 1986 ("Remarks on the Resignation of Supreme Court Chief Justice Warren E. Burger and the Nominations of William H. Rehnquist To Be Chief Justice and Antonin Scalia To Be an Associate Justice," U.S. National Archives and Records Administration, Office of the Federal Register, *Public Papers of the Presidents of the United States: Ronald Reagan, 1986,* vol. 2, p. 781).

[39] Context provides important caveats, as is always the case when exploring median decision-making surrounding Supreme Court nominations. President Eisenhower recessappointed Justice Stewart because Congress was not in session on Oct. 6, 1958 when Justice Burton announced his retirement. The 85th Congress had adjourned *sine die* on Aug. 24, 1958. The President nominated Potter Stewart to the Court on Jan. 17, 1959, after Congress had reconvened for the first session of the 86th Congress. Therefore, although the interval between the starting date (Oct. 6, 1958, as

shown in Table 1) and nomination date (Jan. 17, 1959) is 103 days, and the entire interval from the starting date until final Senate action (May 5, 1959) is 211 days, the President's actual decision-making timetable could also be classified as 8 days, or the interval between Burton's retirement announcement (Oct. 6, 1958) and Eisenhower's recess appointment of Justice Stewart (Oct. 14, 1958). Both intervals are used to calculate the median elapsed time from vacancy to nomination announcement. Nonetheless, the long intervals have a minimal impact on computing the median durations between stages in the process because the median is less sensitive than the mean to extremely high or low values.

[40] For an analysis of the decision-making speed surrounding Supreme Court nominations between 1962-1987, see CRS Report 87-576 GOV, *The Speed With Which Action Has Been Taken on Supreme Court Nominations in the Last 25 Years*, by Denis Steve Rutkus (available from Rutkus).

[41] See, for example, Charles Babington, "Access to Records May Be a Sticking Point; Democrats Push for Prompt Review," *Washington Post*, July 28, 2005, p. A6; and Mike Allen and Jo Becker, "A Clash Over Roberts Documents; Justice Department Balks at Senate Democrats' Demands," *Washington Post*, Aug. 7, 2005, p. A4.

[42] The actual median for the interval between committee final action and Senate action from 1981-2005 is 8.5 days, which is rounded to 9 for the purposes of this report.

[43] The actual median for Senate action from 1900-1980 is 27.5 days, which is rounded to 28 days for the purposes of this report. Median Senate action for 1981-2005 does not include John G. Roberts's Chief Justice confirmation because of the ususal circumstances surrounding the withdrawal of Roberts's nomination for Associate Justice, and his renomination for Chief Justice. The median duration for Senate action when *including* the John G. Roberts Chief Justice confirmation is 81 days (rounded from 80.5) from 1981-2005.

[44] For a profile of Murphy and his death, see *Chicago Daily Tribune*, "Justice Murphy Dies of Heart Attack at 59," *Chicago Daily Tribune*, July 20, 1949, p. 2.

[45] President Truman did not announce that Clark had accepted the nomination until Aug. 1, 1949 (Edward T. Folliard, "Clark Accepts High Court Proffer, *Washington Post*, Aug. 2, 1949, p. 1).

[46] Justice Byron R. White disagreed with the decision. See Ward, *Deciding to Leave*, p. 187.

[47] Tony Mauro, "How Blackmun Hid Retirement Plans," *New Jersey Law Journal,* Apr. 25, 1994, p. 18.

[48] U.S. National Archives and Records Administration, Office of the Federal Register, *Public Papers of the Presidents of the United States: William J. Clinton, 1994,* vol. 1 (Washington: GPO, 1995), p. 597.

[49] U.S. Congress, Joint Committee on Printing, *2003-2004 Official Congressional Directory: 108th Congress* (Washington: GPO), p. 517

[50] "Justice Fuller Dies Suddenly," *Washington Post*, July 5, 1910, p. 1.

[51] In addition to waiting for the Senate to return, President Taft reportedly considered more than 200 nominees, a far more thorough process than the media predicted after Fuller's death (Ibid. and "White Heads Bench," *Washington Post*, Dec. 13, 1910, p. 1).

[52] The discussion of recess appointments in the following two paragraphs is adapted from Rutkus, *Supreme Court Appointments Process*, pp. 15-17.

[53] 53 Adopted by the Senate on Aug. 29, 1960, by a 48-37 vote, S.Res. 334 expressed the sense of the Senate that recess appointments to the Supreme Court "should not be made, except under unusual circumstances and for the purpose of preventing or ending a demonstrable breakdown in the administration of the Court's business." Proponents of the resolution contended, among other things, that judicial independence would be affected if Supreme Court recess appointees, during the probationary period of their appointment, took positions to please the President (in order not to have the President withdraw their nominations) or to please the Senate (in order to gain confirmation of their nominations). It also was argued that Senate investigation of nominations of these recess appointees was made difficult by the oath preventing sitting Justices from testifying about matters pending before the Court. Opponents, however, said, among other things, that the resolution was an attempt to restrict the President's constitutional recess appointment powers and that recess appointments were sometimes called for in order to keep the Court at full strength and to prevent evenly split rulings by its members. See "Opposition to Recess Appointments to the Supreme Court," debate in the Senate on S.Res. 334, *Congressional Record*, vol. 106, Aug. 29, 1960, pp. 18130-18145. See also CRS Report RL31112, *Recess Appointments of Federal Judges,* by Louis Fisher, pp. 16-18.

[54] *U.S. v. Woodley*, 751 F.2d 1008 (9th Cir. 1985).

[55] A notable, relatively recent instance in which the possibility of a recess appointment to the Supreme Court was raised occurred on July 28, 1987, when Senate Minority Leader Robert Dole observed that President Reagan

had the constitutional prerogative to recess appoint U.S. appellate court judge Robert H. Bork to the Court. Earlier that month Judge Bork had been nominated to the Court, and at the time of Senator Dole's statement, the chair of Senate Judiciary Committee, Sen. Joseph R. Biden, Jr. had scheduled confirmation hearings to begin on September 15. With various Republican Senators accusing Senate Democrats of delaying the Bork hearings, Senator Dole offered as "food for thought" the possibility of President Reagan recess appointing Judge Bork during Congress's August recess. See Michael Fumento, "Reagan Has Power To Seat Bork While Senate Stalls: Dole," *Washington Times*, July 28, 1987, p. A3; also, Edward Walsh, "Reagan's Power To Make Recess Appointment Is Noted," *Washington Post*, July 28, 1987, p. A8. Judge Bork, however, did not receive a recess appointment and, as a Supreme Court nominee, was rejected by the Senate in a 58-42 vote on Oct. 23, 1987.

[56] This number does not include instances such as the John G. Roberts *Associate Justice* nomination, in which the Judiciary Committee did not have the opportunity to hold hearings. Hearings before the Judiciary Committee were dispensed with for three nominees: Frank Murphy in 1939, James F. Byrnes in 1941, and Harold H. Burton in 1945, all of whom had prior service in high public office. Murphy had previously served as Governor of Michigan and U.S. Attorney General. Byrnes was a sitting Senator from South Carolina when nominated to the Court. Harold H. Burton was a Senator from Ohio. (Biographical information obtained from the Federal Judicial Center's Federal Judges Biographical Database, available at [http://www.fjc.gov/public/home.nsf/hisj]).

[57] See Rutkus, *Supreme Court Appointment Process*, pp. 17-18.

[58] For additional background information on Senators giving current or former colleagues deference when nominated to the Court, see Rutkus, *Supreme Court Appointments Process*, pp. 17-18.

[59] "White Heads Bench," *Washington Post*, Dec. 13, 1910, p. 1.

[60] Senators Burton and Byrnes's nominations were not referred to the Judiciary Committee. Sen. Black's nomination was referred to the committee, which recommended his confirmation, although by a divided 13-4 vote.

[61] On Stone's testimony before the Judiciary Committee regarding the investigation, see Albert W. Fox, "Stone Tells Senate Committee He Assumes Full Responsibility For Pressing New Wheeler Case," *Washington Post*, Jan. 29, 1925, p. 1.

[62] On increasingly controversial judicial nominations, see chapter 4 in Walter F. Murphy, C. Herman Pritchett, and Lee Epstein, *Courts, Judges, and Politics: An Introduction to the Judicial Process*, 5th ed. (Boston: McGraw Hill, 2002); [Thomas O. Sargentich, Paul D. Carrington, Barbara E. Reed, Charles Gardner Geyh, and Erwin Chemerinsky], *Uncertain Justice: Politics and America's Courts: The Reports of the Task Forces of Citizens for Independent Courts* (New York: The Century Foundation, 2000); and Mark Silverstein, *Judicious Choices: The New Politics of Supreme Court Confirmations* (New York: W.W. Norton and Company, 1994).

[63] The median durations for Senate action shown in Figure 1 and listed in Table 3 do not include the nomination of John G. Roberts as Chief Justice because of the unprecedented circumstances surrounding the nomination. His nomination as Associate Justice was withdrawn, and he was nominated for the Chief Justice position just before the start of his Associate Justice hearing, making the interval between the announcement and first hearing period unusually brief. Had his nomination as Associate Justice proceeded as scheduled, the total amount of time for Senate consideration (from announcement to final Senate action) would have been about 71 days. The median duration for Senate consideration when *including* the John G. Roberts Supreme Court confirmation is 81 days (rounded from the actual median of 80.5), compared with 84 days when *not* including Chief Justice Roberts's confirmation.

INDEX

A

B

C

D

E

V

W